SECRETS
of the
ASCENDED
LIFE

KELLEY
VARNER

DESTINY IMAGE₀ PUBLISHERS, INC.
P.O. Box 310, Shippensburg, PA 17257-0310

*"Speaking to the Purposes of God for this Generation
and for the Generations to Come."*

This book and all other Destiny Image, Revival Press, MercyPlace, Fresh Bread, Destiny Image Fiction, and Treasure House books are available at Christian bookstores and distributors worldwide.

For a U.S. bookstore nearest you, call 1-800-722-6774.
For more information on foreign distributors,
call 717-532-3040.
Or reach us on the Internet: **www.destinyimage.com**

ISBN 10: 0-7684-2358-9

ISBN 13: 978-0-7684-2358-7

For Worldwide Distribution, Printed in the U.S.A.

1 2 3 4 5 6 7 8 9 10 11 / 09 08 07 06

DEDICATION

...there is a friend who sticks closer than a brother (Proverbs 18:24, NIV).

To my companion in tribulation and my co-laborer in the Word of righteousness...

To my friend and brother...

To a man with whom I have traveled in this nation and the nations more than any other...

To a godly husband and father...

To a powerful preacher of great passion and conviction...

To a teacher who is known by many as "The Professor"...

To an anointed scribe and skillful writer...

I proudly dedicate this volume to my close friend and colleague, Apostle Stephen Everett, and his wife Ann.

ACKNOWLEDGMENTS

To Don Milam, for his encouragement to go ahead with this writing, and for his insightful additions to the flow of this manuscript.

To the congregation of Praise Tabernacle of Richlands, North Carolina, for ascending with me in this high calling.

To the Holy Spirit, who is my Teacher.

CONTENTS

FOREWORDS

Dr. Kelley Varner is a true covenant friend and co-laborer in the Kingdom. When I first met this prophet, I heard a man who speaks like I think. He challenged my comfort zones and dared me to come out into the deep with him (Ps. 42:7) to enjoy the *ascended life*. He speaks as one who has sat at the feet of the Master. His books, tapes, and notes always cause me to look at things from the posture of the heavenlies.

Recently, he unveiled the message penned in this book at our Iron Sharpens Iron Men's Conference held yearly in Charlotte, North Carolina. I sat in awe as the atmosphere produced by these truths literally transformed the men right before my eyes.

These prophetic insights will awaken the Church out of its slumber, and cause the hungry to be filled to overflowing. We are not "under the circumstances" looking up at the problem. We are seated in the heavenlies looking at everything from the place of His victory. Our lives are not based on what will happen, but what is already complete *in Him*. We can look through the eyes of God.

I hope that you are ready. This book is about to change your life. Come on up! The view from the *ascended life* is awesome.

Apostle Don Hughes
Impact Church
Iron Sharpens Iron Men's Conference
Regional Pastor, Harvest Churches International

I met Dr. Kelley Varner over eight years ago, and have found him to be a true friend, brother, and mentor in my life and the life of my church family. Dr. Varner has the God-given ability to touch and strengthen God's people, and to bring them to an understanding of revelation and application of a greater truth. As believers, it is our constant desire to be and do better. But our best efforts still come short of living and walking above the problems, struggles, situations, and circumstances that we face in our daily lives.

Dr. Varner's newest book, *Secrets of the Ascended Life*, is a valuable spiritual tool. It helps us to understand that we are not trying to live the Christian life, but rather that Christ is living His life through us. Dr. Varner has declared throughout the Body of Christ for more than three decades that our salvation is an ongoing awareness of what we already possess. This book is instrumental in revealing our rightful position as we are seated in heavenly places far above principalities and powers. Dr. Varner's insight and foresight within the body of Christ conveys to us a greater life in God.

Job 28:7 states, *"There is a path which no fowl knoweth, and which the vulture's eye hath not seen."* A vulture lives on flesh, but there is a life above the flesh that causes us to see as God sees, looking through His eyes.

The prophet Isaiah declared, *"And an highway shall be there, and a way, and it shall be called The way of holiness; the unclean shall not pass over it; but it shall be for those: the wayfaring men, though fools, shall not err therein. No lion shall be there, nor any ravenous beast shall go up thereon, it shall not be found there; but the redeemed shall walk there"* (Isa. 35:8-9). The ascended life is more than just talk. It is a walk, a way of life in God for both our individual and corporate journeys.

God has given Dr. Kelley Varner a voice of being both a proclaimer and an explainer within the Body of Christ. This book clearly proclaims and explains the life of an overcomer. By faith I stand with the author that God has chosen to pen these valuable truths, and by faith I stand with you as the reader of these truths. I believe and pray that God will anoint you and impart to you the ability to live the *ascended life.*

Donald Earl Harrell, Pastor
Rivers of Life Ministries International, Inc.
Macclesfield, North Carolina

PREFACE

I press toward the mark for the prize of the high calling of God in Christ Jesus (Philippians 3:14).

I press on toward the goal to win the [supreme and heavenly] prize to which God in Christ Jesus is calling us upward (Philippians 3:14, AMP).

There *is* a high calling...

Weaving itself like a golden thread throughout the pages of my last book, *Sound the Alarm*, this prophetic declaration provided continuity for that manuscript as it boldly and clearly articulated the apostolic burden of my heart. A fresh exegesis of the Old Testament Book of Joel, and modeled after the Feasts of Jehovah—the Blowing of Trumpets, the Day of Atonement, and the Feast of Tabernacles—that strong Word from the Lord was sent to all my womb-family, "partakers of the heavenly calling" (Heb. 3:1).

Zion is the *"church of the firstborn"* (Heb. 12:23), and Zion also represents the corporate Overcomer within the Church

(Rev. 2-3). The Book of Isaiah presents Zion as a *place*—this is the Most Holy Place in Moses' Tabernacle, *"the secret place of the Most High"* (Ps. 91:1).

Furthermore, Zion is also a *people*, as seen throughout the Book of Psalms. Among many examples, the Bible reveals this overcoming remnant people to be Joel's Army (Joel 2:2-11), the Manchild Company (Rev. 12:1-5), and the 144,000 who stand on Mount Zion, the "firstfruits" unto God and the Lamb (Rev. 14:1-5).

Secrets of the Ascended Life provides a sequel to that previous writing, bringing a clear incentive to ascend the hill of the Lord, the place of the high calling.

I first heard the phrase, "the ascended life," when visiting Evangelist David Wilkerson at his ranch in East Texas in the fall of 1983. He had been listening to several of my cassette tapes and had read my book, *Prevail: A Handbook for the Overcomer.* This world-renowned minister (founder of Teen Challenge) had invited me to spend a week at his guest house for the purpose of sharing with him principles of "present truth" (2 Pet. 1:12).

I fondly remember this hungry man, sitting across the room with a yellow legal pad, writing as fast as I could talk, and both of us shouting over the revelation of God's Word! When I imparted to him the biblical revelation about the overcoming life in Zion and the place of the high calling, he quickly replied, "Pastor Varner, the Lord revealed to me that this is the place of the *ascended life*." I have never forgotten his words...

And He [Jesus] is the head of the body, the church: who is the beginning, the firstborn from the dead; that in all things He might have the preeminence [to be first] (Colossians 1:18).

Everything we teach and minister must be Christo-centric. The Lord Jesus Christ must ever be held high, central, and supreme. The ascended life is *His* life, the life of Him who has already ascended.

We shall discover two powerful Old Testament truths which accentuate and exemplify the ascended life: the *Ascending Offering* (the Burnt Offering), and the *Psalms of Ascent* (Ps. 120-134).

The heart of this manuscript is based upon four messages that I preached at Praise Tabernacle to prepare our local church family for Summer Conference 2005.[1] The theme of that annual gathering was, "Live the High Calling." I shared a four-fold revelation of the ascended life—its *secret*, its *perspective*, its *impartation*, and its *application*. Since then, these truths have burned in my spirit. Thankfully, now they are in print.

And hath raised us up together, and made us sit together in heavenly places in Christ Jesus (Ephesians 2:6).

The *secret* of the ascended life is that we have ascended with Him.

For our conversation [citizenship] *is in heaven; from whence also we look...*(Philippians 3:20).

The *perspective* of the ascended life enables us to look through the eyes of God.

Every good gift and every perfect gift is from above, and cometh down...(James 1:17).

The *impartation* of the ascended life is the downloading of the gift that we are and the gifts that we have. Heaven comes to earth.

But the wisdom that is from above is first pure...(James 3:17).

The application of the ascended life brings to bear the ministry of heavenly wisdom upon earthly situations.

There *is* a high calling....

Ascend Zion's hill with me. What I have heard in the secret place, I now share with you. Get ready. These simple yet profound truths will renew your mind and anoint you for destiny. You are about to be armed and equipped, empowered to look at everyone and everything through the eyes of God.

You are about to be infused with a fresh dose of resurrection life—His life—you are about to learn the *secrets of the ascended life*!

Dr. Kelley Varner
Founder, Praise Tabernacle Ministries
Richlands, North Carolina

ENDNOTE

1. For more information on the Summer Conference 2005, please call 910-324-5026 or e-mail praiztab1@earthlink.net.

Chapter One

THE ASCENDED LIFE
IS HIS LIFE

There *is* a high calling....

Not that I have now attained [this ideal] *or am already made perfect, but I press on to lay hold of (grasp) and make my own, that for which Christ Jesus (the Messiah) has laid hold of me and made me His own.*

I do not consider, brethren, that I have captured and made it my own [yet]; but one thing I do—it is my one aspiration: forgetting what lies behind and straining forward to what lies ahead,

I press on toward the goal to win the [supreme and heavenly] prize to which God in Christ Jesus is calling us upward (Philippians 3:12-14, AMP).

I press toward the mark for the prize of the high [upward] *calling of God in Christ Jesus* (Philippians 3:14). Compare 1 Corinthians 9:24.

The King James Version uses the words "apprehend" and "apprehended" in Philippians 3:12-13. This is the Greek word *katalambano*, which means, "to take eagerly, seize, possess; to lay hold of." It is a compound of the primary preposition *kata* (down) and *lambano* (to take hold of, to have offered to one).

Katalambano reveals the mystery of His incarnation—Jesus came down here and embraced us, apprehended us! He was not intimidated by our sin. He was not afraid to touch us (Heb. 4:14). How low did He go? Jesus has condescended to the lowest human situation (Eph. 4:9-10), where He could touch any person and bring each forth horizontally.

He came down to get me. I didn't find Jesus—He wasn't lost! He found me in a church pew, which was worse than the gutter. I was a religious hypocrite, a church-going sinner. Jesus seized upon me when I was 17, a junior in high school. I have been sovereignly apprehended for the "heavenly calling" (Heb. 3:1), chosen to understand and live the secrets of the ascended life.

We have been "apprehended." Now King Jesus patiently waits for a people to come down, to humble themselves, and eagerly embrace Him with the same intensity and the same passion with which we have been embraced! This is our high calling to worship Him in the Most Holy Place.

> *Therefore shall a man leave his father and his mother, and shall cleave unto his wife: and they shall be one flesh* (Genesis 2:24).

Paul said, *"This one thing I do,"* (Phil. 3:13), and then mentions two things: *"forgetting those things which are behind, **and** *reaching forth unto those things which are before...."* This "one thing" has two aspects. We cannot "cleave" (cling to, stick to, adhere) to our destiny until we "leave" behind (forsake, depart from) our past. We cannot embrace this "new thing" (Isa. 43:19) until we forsake our old paradigms and mindsets. Moses, the old order, is "dead" (Josh. 1:2). It is time for the Joshua generation to arise, cross Jordan, and possess the land!

DEFINITION OF THE HIGH CALLING

Chapters One, Four, and Five of my last book, *Sound the Alarm: The Apocalyptic Message of the Book of Joel*, gives clear definition to this "high calling."

This corporate Overcomer and partaker of the "heavenly calling" (Heb. 3:1) is revealed throughout the Bible. The people of Zion are pictured by these notable Scripture examples:

1. The Joseph Company or Benjamin Company (Genesis 37-50).

2. The Moses-Aaron (King-Priest) Ministry (Exodus 6-12).

3. David's Mighty Men (2 Samuel 23; 1 Chronicles 20).

4. The Elijah Ministry (2 Kings 2).

5. The Shulamite (Song of Solomon 6:8-9).

6. The Saints of the Most High (Daniel 7:18-27).

7. Joel's Army (Joel 2:1-11).

8. The Hundred-fold Company (Matthew 13:23).

9. The Melchisedec Priesthood (Hebrews 5:1-8: 6).

10. The Corporate Overcomer (Revelation 2-3; 21:7).

11. The Manchild Company (Revelation 12:1-5).

12. The 144,000, the Firstfruits Company (Revelation 14:1-5).

The latter two examples are discussed in-depth in Chapter Four of my book, *Moses, the Master, and the Manchild*. Each of these points could become a manuscript, as shown by the Melchizedek Priesthood, the theme of my book, *The More Excellent Ministry*.

THE ASCENDED LIFE

The way of life is above to the wise, that he may depart from hell [death] *beneath* (Proverbs 15:24).

Jesus saith unto him, I am the way, the truth, and the life…(John 14:6).

This high calling, this way or manner of life in the heavens, is the *ascended life*.

The ascended life is *His* life! The purpose for Jesus' incarnation was that "*they* (we) *might have life, and that they* (we) *might have it more abundantly*" (John 10:10). The ascended life, the abundant life, began when we were "born again."

> *Jesus answered, "I tell you the truth, no one can enter the kingdom of God unless he is born of water and the Spirit. Flesh gives birth to flesh, but the Spirit gives birth to spirit. You should not be surprised at My saying, 'You must be born again'"* (John 3:5-7, NIV). Compare John 3:3; 1 Peter 1:23.

The term "born again" is taken from two Greek words. "Born" is the word *gennao*[1] and it means, "to procreate (properly, of the father, but by extension of the mother); figuratively, to regenerate; to be born, be begotten."

"Again" is the word *anothen*[2], and it means, "from above; by analogy, from the first; by implication, anew; from a higher place; used of things which come from heaven or God." It is derived from *ano* (upward or on the top, on high). *Anothen* is used in James 1:17 and James 3:17, the key texts for Chapters Six and Seven of this writing. *Ano* is translated as the "high" calling (Phil. 3:14).

To be "born again" is to be "born from above." Our ascended life in Christ began when we accepted Him as our personal Savior and His blood removed our sin!

> *Who shall ascend into the hill of the Lord? or who shall stand in His holy place?* (Psalm 24:3).

The Hebrew word for "ascend" is *aw-law'*[3]. This primitive root means, "to ascend, intransitively (be high) or actively (mount); to go up, to climb; to spring up; to go up over, to rise; to excel, to be superior to; to offer up." It suggests movement from a lower to a higher place. This is the verb for the noun *o-law'* which is translated as the "burnt offering" (explained fully in the next chapter).

> *Jesus saith unto her, Touch Me not; for I am not yet ascended to My Father: but go to My brethren, and say unto them, I ascend unto My Father, and your Father; and to My God, and your God* (John 20:17).

> *Wherefore He saith, When He [Jesus] ascended up on high, He led captivity captive, and gave gifts unto men.*

(Now that He ascended, what is it but that He also descended first into the lower parts of the earth?

He that descended is the same also that ascended up far above all heavens, that He might fill all things) (Ephesians 4:8-10).

Jesus is the One who ascended and gave gifts unto men (Eph. 4:11). He ascended up "far above" all principality, and power, and might, and dominion (Eph. 1:21)! His is the highest Name (Phil. 2:9; Heb. 1:4)!

The Greek word for "ascend" or "ascended" in these verses is *anabaino*[4]. This compound of *ana* (up) and *basis* (to walk; a pace, a base; the foot) means, "to go up; to rise, to mount, to be borne up, to spring up." It is translated in the King James Version as, "arise, ascend (up), climb (go, grow, rise, spring) up, come (up)."[5]

Thus, to "ascend" is to "walk up" or "step up." The *ascended life*, His life, is a lifestyle or way of life. Step forward so that you can step up! In the Book of Acts, Christians were known as the people of the "way" (Acts 18:25-26; 24:14). That word means, "a road; a progress (the route, act, or distance); figuratively, a mode or means; metaphorically, a course of conduct, a way (that is, manner) of thinking, feeling, deciding." Again, the *ascended life* is a way of life, a lifestyle.

There is a path which no fowl knoweth, and which the vulture's eye hath not seen:

The lion's whelps have not trodden it, nor the fierce lion passed by it (Job 28:7-8).

And a highway will be there; it will be called the Way of Holiness. The unclean will not journey on it; it will be

24

for those who walk in that Way; wicked fools will not go about on it.

No lion will be there, nor will any ferocious beast get up on it; they will not be found there. But only the redeemed will walk there (Isaiah 35:8-9, NIV). Compare Isaiah 40:3; 62:10.

This way of life is the "highway" (thoroughfare, turn-pike, and staircase) of Isaiah's writings.[6] This raised way, this public road, is the highway of the upright (Prov. 16:7). No lion (the devil, as in 1 Pet. 5:8), no lion's whelps (demons), knows or walks that path, that way. It is "far above" them (Eph. 1:21; 4:10)! Interestingly, the word for Jacob's "ladder" in Genesis 28:12, means, "staircase," and is taken from the same root word as "highway." This bottom of Jacob's ladder is this end of Heaven; at the top, the other end of Heaven, is the throne of grace (Matt. 24:31).

Anabaino, the Greek word for "ascend," is also translated in the English Bible as "went up." Jesus, the Pattern Son, often *"went up into a mountain"* (see Matt. 5:1; 14:23; 15:29; Luke 9:28; John 6:3).

The *ascended life*, His life, is the way of life in the heavenlies, and is "far above"[7] all else! We can live "far above" the devil and demons, "far above" the circumstances of life. The old preacher said, "This is so far above that the devil gets a nose-bleed trying to find it!"

The eyes of your understanding being enlightened; that ye may know what is the hope of His calling, and what the riches of the glory of His inheritance in the saints,

And what is the exceeding greatness of His power to us-ward who believe, according to the working of His mighty power,

Which He wrought in Christ, when He raised Him from the dead, and set Him at His own right hand in the heavenly places,

Far above all principality, and power, and might, and dominion, and every name that is named, not only in this world, but also in that which is to come:

And hath put all things under His feet, and gave Him to be the head over all things to the church,

Which is His body, the fulness of Him that filleth all in all (Ephesians 1:18-23).

Can you begin to fathom the weight of the world's sin that Jesus bore on Calvary's cross? Now can you begin to imagine the dimension of power that it would take to raise all of that from the dead? The Holy Ghost demonstrates this power, the power of resurrection life. His is the power by which we are able to live the ascended life!

The Ascended Life is His Life

Know ye not, that so many of us as were baptized into Jesus Christ were baptized into His death?

Therefore we are buried with Him by baptism into death: that like as Christ was raised up from the dead by the glory of the Father, even so we also should walk in newness of life.

For if we have been planted together in the likeness of His death, we shall be also in the likeness of His resurrection

(Romans 6:3-5). Compare Galatians 2:20; 1 Corinthians 15:16-23; Colossians 2:11-12.

When Jesus died, we died with Him. When He was buried, we were buried with Him. When He arose, we arose with Him. And when He ascended, we ascended with Him!

The ascended life is *His* life!

For in Him we live, and move, and have our being...(Acts 17:28).

For it is through union with Him...(Acts 17:28, Goodspeed Bible).

We live and move in Him, can't get away from Him! (Acts 17:28, The Message Bible).

For to me to live is Christ...(Philippians 1:21).

For to me living means Christ...(Philippians 1:21, Williams).

Alive, I'm Christ's messenger...(Philippians 1:21, The Message Bible).

For ye are dead, and your life is hid with Christ in God.

When Christ, who is our life, shall appear, then shall ye also appear with Him in glory (Colossians 3:3-4).

Your old life is dead. Your new life, which is your real *life—even though invisible to spectators—is with Christ in God.* He *is your life* (Colossians 3:3-4, The Message Bible).

When Christ (your real life,) shows up again on this earth, you'll show up, too—the real you, the glorious you...

The Christian life is living the life of Another! We have died, and our life is hidden with Christ in God. When the enemy comes knocking, we send Christ to the door!

The ascended life is *His* life, the life of the One who has ascended up far above all else to fill everything with Himself!

We are not speaking in the mode of the previous order, striving to get the victory. We are not putting this dominion into the future. The ascended life is the life of Him who has already ascended! Jesus is the Ascended One. He that is joined to the Lord is "one spirit" (1 Cor. 6:17). This is not something that we are trying to attain. We are already seated with Him in heavenly places "far above" (Eph. 1:21; 2:6). The hard part isn't getting "up there" or "back there" (in the Most Holy Place). The hard part is coming back down and coming back out!

...I am come that they might have life, and that they might have it more abundantly (John 10:10).

Moreover, the *ascended life* is the life of His abundance. The word "abundantly" here means, "in the sense of beyond, superabundant (in quantity) or superior (in quality); by implication, excessive; over and above, more than is necessary, superadded; superior, extraordinary, surpassing, uncommon pre-eminence, superiority, advantage, more eminent, more remarkable, more excellent"—the high calling!

ABOVE AND BENEATH

There are two kinds of men on this planet: Christ, the new man, and Adam, the old man—beauty and the beast!

And he [Solomon] *said, Lord God of Israel, there is no God like Thee, in heaven above, or on earth beneath, who keepest covenant and mercy with Thy servants that walk before Thee with all their heart* (1 Kings 8:23).

The way of life winds upward for the wise, that he may turn away from hell [death] *below* (Proverbs 15:24, NKJV).

And He [Jesus] *said unto them, Ye are from beneath; I am from above: ye are of this world; I am not of this world* (John 8:23).

The first man is of the earth, earthy: the second man is the Lord from heaven.

As is the earthy, such are they also that are earthy: and as is the heavenly, such are they also that are heavenly.

And as we have borne the image of the earthy, we shall also bear the image of the heavenly (1 Corinthians 15:47-49).

The literal Greek rendering of the latter verse is, "so let us now put on and wear as a garment or a piece of armor the image of the heavenly."

Heaven is from *above*. Earth is from *beneath*.

Christ is from *above*. Adam is from *beneath*.

The fruit of the Spirit is from *above* (Gal. 5:22-24). The works of the flesh are from *beneath* (Gal. 5:19-21).

Righteousness, peace, and joy are from *above* (Rom. 14:17). Unrighteousness, war, and sorrow are from *beneath*.

Sexual sins, evil habits, gluttony and drunkenness, gossip, jealousy, envy, strife, peer pressure, the love of money, power struggles (civil or ecclesiastical), insecurity, any sense of insignificance or inferiority, unrighteous anger, law suits, political correctness, any and all kinds of prejudice, all thoughts of retaliation and revenge, any sort of demonic activity, fear or timidity in any form—all this is from *beneath*—the realm of death and hell (Prov. 15:24).

In Christ, we have been called to live above all the junk and stuff. Preachers, we cannot focus on those lower realms. We cannot speak from beneath—you get what you preach, and you preach what you are. We are to prophesy from the heavens, the place of the ascended life, life more abundantly (John 10:10). We are to bring Heaven to earth (Matt. 6:10).

He is not beneath. He is not "down there" in the lower realms of our whining and complaining, our self-pity, our weakness. This is tough, but He ain't going there! When you throw your pity-party, He will not come, nor will any of His servants. There is nothing "down there" but death and hell.

Are you sick and tired of being bound by earthly things? We can live "down there" in Adam, or "up here" in Christ. We can live the high calling. We can now enjoy the secrets of the ascended life. Choose wisely.

He that cometh from above is above all: he that is of the earth is earthly, and speaketh of the earth: he that cometh from heaven is above all (John 3:31).

The Ascended One and those who live the ascended life in Him are above the cares of life. Stuff is not on top of us. We are on top of it.

Jesus knew that all religion, pictured by the Pharisees of his day, was "beneath" (John 8:23). This adverb is *kato* and it means, "downwards; below." It is also translated in the King

James Version as "bottom, down, under." When Jesus said, "I am from above," He was standing right here on this planet (compare John 3:13). The Message Bible gives a powerful rendering of this truth:

Jesus said, "You're tied down to the mundane; I'm in touch with what is beyond your horizons. You live in terms of what you see and touch. I'm living on other terms.

I told you that you were missing God in all this. You're at a dead end. If you won't believe I am who I say I am, you're at the dead end of sins. You're missing God in your lives" (John 8:23-24, The Message Bible).

But now, by dying to what once bound us, we have been released from the law so that we serve in the new way of the Spirit, and not in the old way of the written code (Romans 7:6, NIV). Compare Romans 6:4.

His death was our death. As new creatures (2 Cor. 5:17), we have now arisen to walk with Him in "newness" (renewal) of life, and serve Him in "newness" of spirit, and not in the oldness of the letter.

That which is born of the flesh is flesh; and that which is born of the Spirit is spirit (John 3:6).

...shall we not much rather be in subjection unto the Father of spirits, and live? (Hebrews 12:9).

As Christians, we are essentially spirit, not human. I am not a human being trying to have a spiritual experience. I am a spirit being of which God Almighty is the Father trying to put up with a human experience. We are eagle saints. We have never fit, and never will. Like God, we are spirit, have a soul, and are expressed through a body. We live in the Spirit, far above. This is the *ascended life.*

> *Since, then, you have been raised with Christ, set your hearts on things above, where Christ is seated at the right hand of God.*
>
> *Set your minds on things above, not on earthly things.*
>
> *For you died, and your life is now hidden with Christ in God* (Colossians 3:1-3, NIV).

Raised Up in the Third Day

Jesus was raised from the dead on the "third day" (Matt. 16:21; Acts 10:40; 1 Cor. 15:3-4).[8]

> *Come, and let us return unto the Lord: for He hath torn, and He will heal us; He hath smitten, and He will bind us up.*
>
> *After two days will He revive us: in the third day He will raise us up, and we shall live in His sight.*
>
> *Then shall we know, if we follow on to know the Lord: His going forth is prepared as the morning; and He shall come unto us as the rain, as the latter and former rain unto the earth* (Hosea 6:1-3).
>
> *But, beloved, be not ignorant of this one thing, that one day is with the Lord as a thousand years, and a thousand years as one day* (2 Peter 3:8).

We are privileged to live in the dawning of a new day. This new day is the Third Day from Jesus and the Seventh Day from Adam (Jude 1:14). This key passage from Hosea heralds the ascended life.

The word for "return" in Hosea 6:1 is *shoob*[9], and it means, "to turn back; again; to bring back, to restore, to refresh, to repair." These are tremendous days of restoration and reformation.

And I will restore to you the years that the locust hath eaten...(Joel 2:25).

From the days of Martin Luther (1517) to the present, the Lord has been restoring to His true Church the years that manmade religious tradition has consumed.

After "two days," after 2,000 years, He has promised to "revive" us. He is quickening us, restoring us to life and health. "In" (during) the Third Day He has determined to "raise us up." He has roused us from sleep and empowered us to stand up again.

Now we "live in His sight," literally, "in His face," His presence. We are ascending. We are being raised up to "follow on," to run after the Lord in the Most Holy Place. We met with Him as our Savior in the Outer Court (Acts 4:12). We experienced Him as Baptizer in the Holy Ghost in the Holy Place (Matt. 3:11; Acts 1:5; 2:1-4). Now we meet with Him yet a third time as Lord as He raises us up in the Feast of Tabernacles (Deut. 16:16).

The ascended life is *His* life. The virtue of the indwelling Christ (Col. 1:27) empowers us to ascend into the heights of Zion.

The ascended life is the high calling. The ascended life is *His* life. Christ is from above. Adam is from beneath. God is raising us up in the Third Day.

The ascended life is revealed throughout both Testaments. Every major Old Testament type points to Jesus, the ascended One. He is the Antitype, the fulfillment of every Old Testament shadow. Jesus is the Substance. He is the once-for-all Offering that consummates every Old Testament sacrifice, especially the Burnt Offering, less commonly known as the *Ascending Offering*.

ENDNOTES

1. James Strong. *Strong's Dictionary of Bible Words* (New York, New York: Nelson Reference, 1996), #1080.

2. Ibid., #509.

3. Ibid., #5927.

4. Ibid., #305.

5. *Anabaino,* the Greek word for "ascend," is translated in the King James Version as "arise" (Luke 24:38; Rev. 9:2; 19:3); "ascend" or "ascend up" or "ascending" (see Luke 19:28; John 1:51; 3:13; 6:62; 20:17; Acts 2:34; 25:1; Rom. 10:6; Eph. 4:8-10; and Rev. 7:2; 8:4; 11:7,12; 14:11; 17:8); "climb up" (Luke 19:4; John 10:1); and "grow up" (Mark 4:7,32). There are also numerous references translated as "went up" or "go up" or "come up."

6. The ascended life is the "highway" of Isaiah's writings (Isa. 7:3; 11:16; 19:23; 35:8; 36:2; 40:3; and 62:10). The same word is also used in Jeremiah 31:21.

7. I have chosen the terminology, the *ascended life,* to describe the high calling. Besides the word "ascend," other key words which help us understand this truth are "far above" or "above." Note these additional verses about His life lived "from above": We have been born again, literally, "from above" (John 3:7); He (and we) that comes "from above" (Heaven) is above all (John 3:31); those "from above" are not of this world (John 8:23 with 1 John 2:15-17); all power (authority) is given "from above" (John 19:11); the Jerusalem "from above" is our mother (Gal. 4:26); His Name "from above" is above all other names (Phil. 2:9); we seek those things which are "above" (Col. 3:1-2); every good and

perfect gift is "from above" (James 1:17); and our wisdom in Christ is "from above" (James 3:15-17).

8. An in-depth teaching concerning the Third Day is set forth in my book, *The Priesthood Is Changing*.

9. Strong, #7725.

Chapter Two

The Ascending Offering

There *is* a high calling! This heavenly calling is the *ascended life*. The ascended life is *His* life (Acts 17:28; Phil. 1:21; Col. 3:3-4).

There are two major pictures of this in the Old Testament:

1. The Burnt Offering, also known as the *Ascending Offering*.

2. The *Psalms of Ascent* (Ps. 120-134).

This chapter reveals the Person of the Ascended One in the most important offering of all: the Ascending Offering.

Basic Truths About the Offerings

The importance of the Old Testament offerings is indicated by the many chapters devoted to the subject (Lev. 1-7), and by the many references thereto in other Scriptures. These offerings were communicated by Jehovah through Moses as revelatory truth.

Unto Adam also and to his wife did the Lord God make coats of skins, and clothed them (Genesis 3:21).

The word for "coats" (to cover) here is also used for Joseph's coat of many colors (Gen. 37) and the coats for Aaron and his sons ((Ex. 28-29). This institution (the first act) of sacrifice in Genesis 3 was performed by God for the purpose of relieving humankind's conscience from its sense of guilt and shame. The provision of a covering for the bodies of our first parents was Jehovah's answer for the covering of humankind's sins, and for the mending of the break of fellowship between God and man caused by sin.

For the life of the flesh is in the blood: and I have given it to you upon the altar to make an atonement for your souls: for it is the blood that maketh an atonement for the soul (Leviticus 17:11).

And almost all things are by the law purged with blood; and without shedding of blood is no remission [forgiveness] (Hebrews 9:22). Compare Ephesians 1:7.

Since the life of the flesh is in the blood, blood must be shed for the atonement of life. Man is doomed as a sinner (Rom. 3:10,23; 6:23), but God has purposed to save him. The life has been forfeited as a result of sin; the sin-debt requires that man should die. But God appoints a way of escape and appoints a substitute—another life is to be given for the life of man!

This way of life is through death! The only way of approach unto God is by means of sacrifice and blood. Therefore, in the Mosaic economy, the sacrifices of the Tabernacle were the pivotal point around which its service revolved. Every Old Testament offering pointed ahead to the

Person and Work of the Lord Jesus Christ, for He is the *"Lamb without blemish* [flaw, blot] *and without spot* [stain, soil]" (1 Pet. 1:19).

> *The next day John seeth Jesus coming unto him, and saith, Behold the Lamb of God, which taketh away* [lift up and bear away] *the sin of the world* (John 1:29).

The efficacy of the Old Testament animal sacrifices was limited. They covered sin, but could not remove sin. That old order was marked by the remembrance of sin; it had to be dealt with annually during the Day of Atonement (Lev. 16). The underlying dynamic that gave animal sacrifices their efficacy, their power to cover sin, was the perfect sacrifice of Jesus Christ foreordained before the foundation of the world (1 Pet. 1:18-20; Rev. 13:8)!

There were five primary Levitical offerings (the number for grace). Compare Jesus' five bleeding points at the Cross—His hands, feet, and side. These five offerings were divided into two categories.

> *...it is a burnt sacrifice, an offering made by fire, of a sweet savour unto the Lord* (Leviticus 1:17). Compare Leviticus 2:9; 3:6,16.

First, there were three Sweet Savour Offerings—the Burnt Offering, the Meal Offering, and the Peace Offering. These were voluntary, and speak of *worship*. The word *sweet* means, "restful, pleasant, soothing, quieting, tranquilizing; delight." The word *savour* means, "scent, odor, or aroma (as if blown)."

> *And walk in love, as Christ also hath loved us, and hath given Himself for us an offering and a sacrifice to God for*

a sweetsmelling [good fragrance, well-pleasing]
savour...(Ephesians 5:2).

The Burnt, Meal, and Peace Offerings are called "sweet savour" offerings because they typify Jesus Christ offering Himself without sin (spot) to God in delight to do His Father's will even unto death. Here His finished work is viewed *Godward*, what the Person and Work of the Son was to the Father, namely, a delightful fragrance!

When you were dead in your sins and in the uncircumcision of your sinful nature, God made you alive with Christ. He forgave us all our sins, (Colossians 2:13, NIV).

Second, there were two Non-sweet Savour Offerings—the Sin Offering and the Trespass Offering. These were involuntary or required of all, and speak of *the forgiveness of sin*.

These two offerings made reparation and satisfaction for the offense and expiation of sin. This work is *manward*, for they picture Jesus Christ's identifying Himself with the sinner, and offering Himself for us to God as our representative for sin. His was a vicarious sacrifice.

To summarize, in the Sweet Savour Offerings, the offerer came as a *devoted worshiper*. In the Non-sweet Savour Offerings, he came as a *convicted sinner*. In the former, Jesus Christ presented Himself for us to God *without sin*; in the latter, Jesus offered Himself as our representative *for sin*. In the former, there is revealed the preciousness of the sacrifice; in the latter, we understand the heinousness of the sin.

The most significant of all the five offerings was the Burnt Offering, or the *Ascending Offering*. It points to the Ascended One and His life, and affords us one of the secrets of the ascended life.

The Ascending Offering

The Burnt Offering is the Ascending Offering. The previous chapter revealed the ascended life to be *His* life. The Burnt Offering or the Ascending Offering (Ex. 29:38-46; Lev. 1:1-17; 6:8-13) is an amazing revelation of His high calling.

As noted, the Hebrew word for "ascend" is *aw-law'*, and it means, "to ascend, go up, climb; be high, to mount; to excel, to be superior to; to exalt; to be taken up into."

The word rendered as "burnt offering" is in the same family. It is *o-law'*[1], and it means, "a step or (collectively, stairs, as ascending); usually a holocaust (as going up in smoke); an ascent, stairway." The Burnt Offering is the *Ascending Offering.*

And Melchizedek king of Salem brought forth bread and wine: and he was the priest of the most high God.

And he blessed him, and said, Blessed be Abram of the most high God, possessor of heaven and earth:

And blessed be the most high God, which hath delivered thine enemies into thy hand. And he [Abram] gave him tithes of all (Genesis 14:18-22).

The name *Elyon* (highest or uppermost) is from the same root. *El-Elyon* means, "the most high God." This was the God of Melchizedek, the mysterious one who prefigures Jesus as prophet, priest, and king (Heb. 5:1-8:6). This directly ties in with those who have been apprehended for the high calling, for we are a "royal priesthood" (1 Pet. 2:9). Having been made kings and priests unto our God, we shall reign on the earth (Rev. 1:6; 5:10).

But made Himself nothing, taking the very nature of a servant, being made in human likeness.

And being found in appearance as a man, He humbled himself and became obedient to death—even death on a cross!

Therefore God exalted Him to the highest place and gave Him the name that is above every name (Philippians 2:7-9, NIV).

The Ascending Offering is a picture of Jesus Christ offering Himself without spot to God in complete delight to do His Father's will, even unto death (Ps. 40:6-8). This offering reveals the perfect obedience and consecration of the Ascended One to God the Father. Jesus was the Man for whom God sought (Ezek. 22:30), the One who at last would fully glorify God in all things (John 8:28-29; 17:4)! As noted in the description given below, God got *everything* in the Burnt Offering. Jesus gave it *all*!

These same truths find corporate expression and manifestation in those who are called to the same high (upward) calling, the brethren of whom He is not ashamed (Rom. 8:14-23; Heb. 2:6-13). Those called to be partakers of His image and likeness are to receive the benefits of His abundant, ascended life (John 10:10).

THE APPOINTED SACRIFICES

The appointed sacrifices of the Ascending Offering were revealed in three dimensions. This illustrates the principle of "excellent" or *"three-fold"* things (Prov. 22:20-21).[2]

Note this chart:

Outer Court	Holy Place	Most Holy Place
Passover	Pentecost	Tabernacles
Born Again	Spirit-filled	Mature

All man	God and man	All God
External	Internal	Eternal
Thanksgiving	Praise	Worship
30-fold	60-fold	100-fold
Out of Egypt	Through the Wilderness	Into the land

Moreover, the five offerings themselves can be listed among these three dimensions. The Sin Offering and the Trespass Offering relegate themselves to the Outer Court; the Brazen Altar was the only place where sin was dealt with.

The Meal Offering and the Peace Offering line up with the Holy Place; indeed, the Table of Shewbread *was* a Meal Offering.

But the Burnt Offering, the Ascending Offering, was the highest order of the five and pertains to the Most Holy Place, the place of the high calling. Just as God revealed Himself in the tabernacle from the inside out, giving instructions *first* about the Ark of the Covenant in the Holy of Holies (Ex. 25:8-22), so the Ascending Offering is listed *first* among all the sacrifices (Lev. 1:1-17). These examples typify a people in Zion who are known as the "firstfruits" unto God and the Lamb (Rev. 14:1-5).

Furthermore, the Burnt Offering had three levels of sacrifice for the people of Israel. With regard to the various sacrifices of the Ascending Offering, compare these categories:

Lower class	Middle class	Upper class
Turtledove, pigeon	Sheep, goat	Bullock

Where no oxen are, the crib is clean: but much increase is by the strength of the ox (Proverbs 14:4). See also Psalm 144:14.

From God's standpoint, these appointed sacrifices began with the highest level of giving, a bullock or ox (young bull). This was literally, "a son of the herd" (Lev. 1:5). This reveals the prompt and ready attitude of the ascended Christ, ever prepared for service and sacrifice. Pictured by the ox, Jesus is the Servant of Jehovah (Isa. 42:1-5), as revealed in Mark's Gospel, the strong One who is humble, patient, gentle, and powerful. All those apprehended for the ascended life are called to be like Him.

And if his offering be of the flocks, namely, of the sheep, or of the goats, for a burnt sacrifice; he shall bring it a male without blemish (Leviticus 1:10).

Next was a sheep or a goat. The sheep points to the patient submission of the Lamb of God (Acts 8:32-33 with John 1:29). Jesus was the subjected One. As seen below, the daily Burnt Offering was a male lamb of the first year. This goat reveals the planned substitution of Jesus Christ, our Sin-bearer and Scapegoat.

And if the burnt sacrifice for his offering to the Lord be of fowls, then he shall bring his offering of turtledoves, or of young pigeons (Leviticus 1:14).

Finally, the turtledove or young pigeon could be offered. This reveals the patient sincerity of the One who is our consummate Burnt Offering. This is Jesus the sorrowing One (Isa. 38:14; 53:3-4; 59:11; Matt. 26:37-38), whose character has no guile or deceit (Matt. 10:16; 1 Pet. 2:22; Rev. 14:5).

And every oblation of thy meat offering shalt thou season with salt; neither shalt thou suffer the salt of the covenant of thy God to be lacking from thy meat offering:

with all thine offerings thou shalt offer salt (Leviticus 2:13).

Let your speech be always with grace, seasoned with salt, that ye may know how ye ought to answer every man (Colossians 4:6).

Salt was added to the Ascending Offering (Ezek. 43:24), and speaks of grace. Jesus came to reveal grace and truth (John 1:14,17). Salt is a preservative and has an action opposing corruption (Acts 13:33-37). Salt became a symbol of hospitality, durability, and fidelity in that it also speaks of covenant (Lev. 2:13; 2 Chron. 13:5; Mark 9:49-50).

THE CONTINUAL BURNT OFFERING

The regular Ascending Offering discussed above could be offered at any time, but the Continual Burnt Offering (Ex. 29:36-46; Lev. 6:8-13) was different. This perpetual sacrifice was offered each day, morning and evening. The Continual Ascending Offering, also called the "whole burnt offering" (Deut. 33:10; Ps. 51:19) and "the daily sacrifice" (Dan. 8:11-13; 11:31; 12:11), was instituted upon the induction of Aaron and sons to the priesthood.

...He hath made us accepted [graced, favored] *in the beloved* (Ephesians 1:6).

The primary purpose of this continual offering was a daily reminder to Israel of their abiding acceptance with God based upon His foresight of the Sacrifice to come. It was on this ground that God met with, spoke to, and dwelt in the midst of His redeemed people. Thus is revealed our position in Christ.

The fire on the altar must be kept burning; it must not go out. Every morning the priest is to add firewood and arrange the burnt offering on the fire...(Leviticus 6:12, NIV).

...it shall not be put out [expire; to quench or extinguish]...(Leviticus 6:12).

For by one offering He hath perfected for ever them that are sanctified (Hebrews 10:14).

The fire on the altar was never to go out. This vividly describes the ever-abiding efficacy of Jesus' once-for-all blood sacrifice of Himself on the Cross. Our Savior's finished work affords the believer a perpetual standing in acceptance with God! The fire was to ever burn brightly! His love for us never ceases (1 Cor. 13:8-13)!

And I looked, and, lo, a Lamb stood on the mount Sion, and with Him an hundred forty and four thousand, having His Father's name written in their foreheads (Revelation 14:1).

Two first-year lambs were offered daily (Ex. 29:39,41). This points to Jesus the Lamb of God (John 1:29) and to the corporate Overcomer, the Lamb Company conformed to His image (Rev. 14:1-5)!

One lamb was offered in the morning and the other in the evening. Jesus was offered at the beginning of this age. Those with His lamb-like nature apprehended for the ascended life appear at the end of this age. Jesus fulfills the type of the morning lamb. Like the twin corner boards of Moses' Tabernacle (Ex. 26:23-24), and the twin pillars of Solomon's Temple (1 Kings 7:21), there is now in the earth another lamb just like the first Lamb!

God Gets Everything

In the Ascending Offering, Jehovah God received the whole of the flayed and jointed sacrifice. In the presentation of the Ascending Offering, God gets *all* of it. This reveals the 100 percent commitment of the Pattern Son and the 100-fold Company who are His brethren.

The word for "whole burnt offering" is *kaw-leel'*[3], and it means, "complete; as a noun, the whole (specifically, a sacrifice entirely consumed); as an adverb, fully." It also means, "entire, all, perfect; holocaust, entirety." This is the "whole offering." It is also translated as "wholly burnt" (Lev. 6:22-23), and as "whole burnt sacrifice" (Deut. 33:10). God got everything, the "whole" offering!

> *And walk in love, as Christ also has loved us and given Himself for us, an offering and a sacrifice to God for a sweet-smelling aroma* (Ephesians 5:2, NKJV).

The whole Burnt Offering finds its antitype, its fulfillment, in the New Testament with regard to Jesus and His Church. Jesus is the "sweet-smelling aroma" offered up to God as the Pattern Son, the One who completely delighted to do the Father's will (Ps. 40:6-8). The ascended life is *His* life. We are being conformed to His image.

> *For Thou desirest not sacrifice; else would I give it: Thou delightest not in burnt offering.*
>
> *The sacrifices of God are a broken spirit: a broken and a contrite heart, O God, Thou wilt not despise* (Psalm 51:16-17).
>
> *I beseech you therefore, brethren, by the mercies of God, that ye present your bodies a living sacrifice, holy, acceptable unto God, which is your reasonable service.*

And be not conformed to this world: but be ye transformed by the renewing of your mind, that ye may prove what is that good, and acceptable, and perfect, will of God (Romans 12:1-2).

His glorious Church has been born from above and apprehended for the ascended life. We can only become a whole burnt offering as we allow the King to live His overcoming life in and through us. Greatly limited by our own wisdom or strength, we must be energized by His Spirit (Zech. 4:6; Rom. 8:14)! Our being a "living sacrifice" is the living out of His life from within!

I press toward the mark for the prize of the high [upward] *calling of God in Christ Jesus* (Philippians 3:14).

The whole Burnt Offering, the Ascending Offering, is a powerful picture of the high calling! This heavenly summons is the upward drawing by the Holy Spirit to the top of Mount Zion. The word for "prize" in this verse is *brabeion*, and it means, "an award (of arbitration), (specially) a prize to the victor in the public games." It is only used in one other reference. To all those who are called up to Zion—finish strong!

Know ye not that they which run in a race run all, but one receiveth the prize? So run, that ye may obtain (1 Corinthians 9:24).

Again, we are not equal to the task of the high calling, but the One who lives within has already made the dedication, having completely surrendered Himself to do the Father's will with delight. Loose Him and let Him go! The living sacrifice of the Christian life, the fulfillment of the

Ascending Offering, is the living out of His life from the nature of the Lamb within!

> *I am* [have been] *crucified with Christ: nevertheless I live; yet not I, but Christ liveth in me: and the life which I now live in the flesh I live by the faith of the Son of God, who loved me, and gave Himself for me* (Galatians 2:20).

In the "whole burnt offering," the "daily sacrifice," Jesus is both Offerer and Minister! We can live like the offered Lamb morning and evening because of His faith to agree with the Father. His faith for complete obedience, even His faith to conquer the last enemy, is already at work in the people who have ascended into Zion!

ENDNOTES

1. James Strong. *Strong's Dictionary of Bible Words* (New York, New York: Nelson Reference, 1996), #5930.

2. My book, *Prevail: A Handbook for the Overcomer* (pages 84-85), gives over 40 examples of these "three-fold" things (Prov. 22:20-21).

3. Strong, #3632.

Chapter Three

THE PSALMS OF ASCENT

There *is* a high calling! This high calling is the *ascended life*.

The ascended life is *His* life (Acts 17:28; Phil. 1:21; Col. 3:3-4).

Again, the Old Testament models this in two major ways:

1. The Burnt Offering, also known as the *Ascending Offering*.

2. The *Psalms of Ascent* (Ps. 120-134).

The previous chapter unfolded in depth the truths concerning the highest offering, the Burnt Offering, also known as the Ascending Offering. Jesus Christ is the consummate Worshiper. His apprehended family is created in His image and likeness. His end-time Church will constitute a corporate sacrifice.

SECRETS OF THE ASCENDED LIFE

Now we turn our attention to the other significant picture of the ascended life in the Old Testament—the 15 Songs of Degrees, the *Psalms of Ascent*.

THE SONGS OF DEGREES

The name "Songs of Degrees" is based upon a phrase that occurs in the titles of 15 psalms, Psalms 120-134—"A Song of Degrees." The Amplified Bible uses the words, "A Song of Ascents." In the King James Version, Psalms 122, 124, 131, and 133 are additionally titled, "A Song of Degrees of David;" and Psalm 127 carries the inscription, "A Song of Degrees for Solomon."

These 15 songs, Psalms 120-134, bear the Hebrew inscription, *Shir Hama'aloth.* "Ascents" translates the Hebrew word *ma'aloth*, which means, "goings up." The Latin Vulgate calls them, *Canticum graduum.* Martin Luther referred to them as, "a song of the higher choir." One Hebrew rendering is, "songs of the pilgrim caravans," or "on the homeward marches." The correct Hebrew translation for each of these 15 psalms is, "Song of the Ascent."

The Hebrew word for "degrees" (2 Kings 20:8-11; Isa. 38:8) is *mah-al-aw'*[1], and it means, "elevation, the act (literally, a journey to a higher place, figuratively, a thought arising), or (concretely) the condition (literally, a step or grade-mark, figuratively, a superiority of station); specifically a climactic progression (in certain Psalms)." It is the feminine form of *mah-al-eh'*[2], which means, "an elevation, (concretely) acclivity or platform; abstractly (the relation or state) a rise or (figuratively) priority; an ascent, an incline."

Both these words are from the root *aw-law'* (to ascend). These words provide a vivid description of the Ascended One and those who partake of His life.

The Songs of Degrees are also known as:

1. The Gradual Psalms.

2. The Pilgrim Psalms.

3. The Songs of the Goings Up.

4. The Songs of the Journeyings Up.

5. The Songs of the Steps.

6. The Ascent Psalms or the *Psalms of Ascent*.

There were 15 Songs of Degrees. Fifteen is the biblical numbering denoting rest.[3]

THE OCCASIONS FOR THE SONGS OF DEGREES

...thou shalt go up [ascend] *to appear before the Lord thy God thrice in the year* (Exodus 34:24). Compare 1 Samuel 1:3; 1 Kings 12:27.

Three times in a year shall all thy males appear before the Lord thy God in the place which He shall choose; in the feast of unleavened bread [Passover, in the first month], *and in the feast of weeks* [Pentecost, in the third month], *and in the feast of tabernacles* [in the seventh month]: *and they shall not appear before the Lord empty* (Deuteronomy 16:16).

And you will sing as on the night you celebrate a holy festival; your hearts will rejoice as when people go up with flutes to the mountain of the Lord, to the Rock of Israel (Isaiah 30:29, NIV).

These songs were chanted by the caravans of the people of God as they went up (ascended) to Jerusalem to keep the three annual Feasts of Passover, Pentecost, and Tabernacles (Lev. 23). Thus they are known as the Ascent Psalms, sung by worshipers who ascend the hill of the Lord. We sing as we ascend.

Speaking to yourselves in psalms and hymns and spiritual songs, singing and making melody in your heart to the Lord (Ephesians 5:19). Compare Colossians 3:16.

The marks of a genuinely Spirit-filled life are that we are always singing, always thankful, and always submitted one to the other (Eph. 5:17-20).

Our growth in grace is an ongoing awareness of who we already are in Christ on the basis of what He has already done in His finished work—His death, burial, resurrection, ascension, and coronation. The song of the Lord is our strength as we go. The ascended life is a life of song.

Who is there among you of all His people? his God be with him, and let him go up to Jerusalem, which is in Judah, and build the house of the Lord God of Israel, (He is the God,) which is in Jerusalem.

Then rose up the chief of the fathers of Judah and Benjamin, and the priests, and the Levites, with all them whose spirit God had raised, to go up [ascend] to build the house of the Lord which is in Jerusalem (Ezra 1:3,5).

The Psalms of Ascent were no doubt sung by the people of the post-exilic restoration as they returned to Jerusalem from the captivity in Babylon (confusion). Thus they are called the Pilgrim Songs. From the days of Martin Luther (1517) to the present, God has been restoring to His Church the years that the locusts of dark, religious tradition have eaten (Joel 2:25). Every major move of God from the First Reformation until now has had its own song. With every new progressive day, there is a corresponding sound and song. There is a new song in this Third Day.

> *And David went up, and all Israel, to Baalah, that is, to Kirjath-jearim, which belonged to Judah, to bring up [ascend] thence the ark of God the Lord, that dwelleth between the cherubims, whose name is called on it* (1 Chronicles 13:6).

> *So David, and the elders of Israel, and the captains over thousands, went to bring up [ascend] the ark of the covenant of the Lord out of the house of Obed-edom with joy* (1 Chronicles 15:25).

> *Then Solomon assembled the elders of Israel, and all the heads of the tribes, the chief of the fathers of the children of Israel, unto Jerusalem, to bring up [ascend] the ark of the covenant of the Lord out of the city of David, which is Zion* (2 Chronicles 5:2).

King David, and later King Solomon, sung these songs of degrees as they brought the Ark of the Covenant up to Jerusalem and to Zion. Thus they are called the Songs of the Goings Up. The Ark has to do with the Most Holy Place, the place of the high calling. It would require a separate study to compare David's ascent into Zion with Jesus' ascent to the right hand of the Father (Ps. 24 with John 20:17; Acts 2:34-35; Eph. 4:8-10: also compare 2 Sam. 15:23,30 with John 18:1).

> *Let the saints be joyful in glory: let them sing aloud upon their beds.*

Let the high praises of God be in their mouth...(Psalm 149:5-6).

It is quite possible that each title, "A Song of Ascents," references to some peculiarity in connection with the music itself, or the manner of playing or singing it. Perhaps these high praises were sung in a higher key (degree) or with an elevated voice.

There are several other considerations for the application of truth regarding these 15 Songs of Degrees.

Then came he unto the gate which looketh toward the east, and went up the stairs thereof... (Ezekiel 40:6).

The gateway and its portico had narrow openings all around, like the openings of the others. It was fifty cubits long and twenty-five cubits wide.

Seven steps led up to it...

(The porticoes of the gateways around the inner court were twenty-five cubits wide and five cubits deep.)

Its portico faced the outer court; palm trees decorated its jambs, and eight steps led up to it (Ezekiel. 40:25-26,30-31, NIV).

First, there were a total of 15 steps (seven steps plus eight steps) *going up* by which the priests ascended into the Temple described by the prophet Ezekiel. This pictures the stability and the permanency of the Temple concept, and also points ahead to Jesus' New Testament Melchisedec priesthood (Heb. 5:1-8:6). Jesus' king-priest ministry, the "royal priesthood" (1 Pet. 2:9), parallels the Zadok (righteous) priesthood in Ezekiel, and fulfills the type of the "faithful priest" (1 Sam. 2:36).

And the very God of peace sanctify you wholly; and I pray God your whole spirit and soul and body be preserved blameless unto the coming of our Lord Jesus Christ (1 Thessalonians 5:23).

Second, the Jewish Mishnah records that 15 steps led up from the Court of the Women to the Court of the Israelites (men), and upon them the Levites used to stand and sing. This ascent of the soul (feminine) unto the spirit (masculine) would require a separate study.

And there were six steps to the throne, with a footstool of gold, which were fastened to the throne, and stays on each side of the sitting place, and two lions standing by the stays:

And twelve lions stood there on the one side and on the other upon the six steps. There was not the like made in any kingdom (2 Chronicles 9:18-19).

Third, the first seven of the Psalms of Ascent are pictured by the steps of King Solomon's throne (the throne being the seventh level). Parallel that with the seven churches of Revelation 2-3, leading to the throne, the place of rulership (Rev. 3:21). One could also compare the seven things we add to our faith, mentioned in Second Peter 1:4-9, or the seven days of creation (Gen. 1).

SALVATION IS PROGRESSIVE[4]

Who delivered us from so great a death, and doth deliver: in whom we trust that He will yet deliver us (2 Corinthians 1:10).

The Greek noun for "salvation" is *soteria*. The verb is *sozo*. This is simple yet profound: our "salvation" is a "complete deliverance." Salvation is progressive. Our spirit has been saved (Col. 1:9-13), our soul is being saved, our mind is being renewed (Heb. 10:38-39), and our body shall be saved (Phil. 3:21).

From strength to strength (Ps. 84:7), from faith to faith (Rom. 1:17), and from glory to glory (2 Cor. 3:18), we are being changed. The secret of the ascended life, as revealed throughout the Psalms of Degrees, is the life of transformation.

To live is to grow. To grow is to change. Apostle G.C. McCurry,[5] one of my mentors, taught me that "spiritual growth denotes change after change after change."

And was transfigured before them: and His face did shine as the sun, and His raiment was white as the light (Matthew 17:2). Compare Mark 9:2.

And be not conformed to this world: but be ye trans-formed by the renewing of your mind, that ye may prove what is that good, and acceptable, and perfect, will of God (Romans 12:2).

But we all, with open face beholding as in a glass the glory of the Lord, are changed into the same image from glory to glory, even as by the Spirit of the Lord (2 Corinthians 3:18).

The word translated as "transfigured," "transformed," and "changed," in these verses is the Greek verb *metamorphoo*, and it means, "to change into another form, to transform." It is derived from *meta* (change) and *morphoo* (to form, fashion). The 15 Psalms of Ascent, a revelation of the ascended life, have to do with our growth, movement, progression, maturity, change, formation, development, restoration, repentance (change of mind), and transfiguration.

58

For whom He did foreknow, He also did predestinate to be conformed to the image of His Son, that He [Jesus] might be the firstborn among many brethren (Romans 8:29).

Biblical sonship has to do with our maturing in Christ. For example, the epistle to the Galatians has as its theme the maturation of the seed (Gal. 3:7,9,16,29; 4:6,19).

We are being conformed to the image of Jesus Christ. We are ascending into the higher realms of the Spirit. We are returning to the dominion in Eden, and to the bosom of the Father. We are being changed. We are being saved (delivered), growing in the grace and knowledge of our Lord Jesus Christ. We are ascending into Zion and the full authority of His throne, the hill of the Lord. Our salvation is progressive. We are becoming just like Jesus!

Who may ascend the hill of the Lord? Who may stand in His holy place?

He who has clean hands and a pure heart, who does not lift up his soul to an idol or swear by what is false.

He will receive blessing from the Lord and vindication from God his Savior.

Such is the generation of those who seek Him, who seek Your face, O God of Jacob. Selah (Psalm 24:3-6, NIV).

THE SECRET PLACES OF THE STAIRS

The steps of a good man are ordered by the Lord: and He delighteth in his way (Psalm 37:23).

Order my steps in Thy word... (Psalm 119:133).

We learned in the last chapter that there are three dimensions or levels in our Christian maturity, as revealed by the

Outer Court, the Holy Place, and the Most Holy Place of Moses' Tabernacle. The three Feasts of Jehovah—Passover, Pentecost, and Tabernacles—parallel these truths. In Christ, we are babes and youths, then men—little children, young men, and fathers (1 John 2:12-14).

> *The entrance to the lowest floor was on the south side of the temple; a stairway* [spiral steps, staircase] *led up to the middle level and from there to the third* (1 Kings 6:8, NIV).

These three dimensions of grace are clearly seen in the "winding stairs" that went up into the three levels of Solomon's Temple. Solomon made reference to this in his Song of Songs.

> *O my dove, that art in the clefts of the rock, in the secret places of the stairs, let me see thy countenance, let me hear thy voice; for sweet is thy voice, and thy countenance is comely* (Song of Solomon 2:14).

The word for "stairs" in this verse means, "a step; a steep or inaccessible place." Note these other translations:

...in the hiding places on the mountainside... (NIV)

...in the secret places of the cliff... (NKJV)

...in the sheltered and secret place of the cliff... (AMP)

...in a secret place of the ascent... (Young's Literal)

The devil can't get there. Demons can't get there. Adam can't get there. The only one who can ascend is Christ!

We are in union with the ascended One. Like the Dove, we are a Spirit-filled, single-eyed Church. We are safe and secure in the clefts of the Rock, *in* Christ. Now we can move up the secret places of the stairs and ascend *into* Christ. In this elevated position, His voice has become our voice, and His face has become our face (face to face)! God loves to listen to Himself, and to look at Himself. There is no spot in Him, and now, because of His blood, there is no spot in us (Song of Solomon 4:7)!

> *After this I looked, and, behold, a door was opened in heaven: and the first voice which I heard was as it were of a trumpet talking with me; which said, Come up hither [here]...(Revelation 4:1).*

> *And there came one of the seven angels which had the seven vials, and talked with me, saying unto me, Come hither [here]...(Revelation 17:1).* Compare Revelation 21:9.

Compare this invitation of Song of Solomon 2:14 with John's experience in the Revelation. "Come up here"—get *in* Christ and His ascended life. Then "come here"—get *into* Christ by a progressive lifestyle of worship.

The ascended life is living His life in the secret place. This is the life of love, of intimate union and communion with the Lord. It is the life of our bridal affection for our Bridegroom Lover. Jesus is our Beloved. We are safe and secure in Him.

> *He that dwelleth in the secret place of the most High shall abide under the shadow of the Almighty* (Psalm 91:1). Compare Psalms 18:11; 81:7.

> *And I will give thee the treasures of darkness, and hidden riches of secret places, that thou mayest know that I, the Lord, which call thee by thy name, am the God of Israel* (Isaiah 45:3).

God orders our steps onward and upward as we are born again (John 3:7), Spirit-filled (Acts 2:4), and then mature, full-grown (Eph. 4:13).

He desires to meet with us in Christ three times (Deut. 16:16). As we ascend, there is room at the cross for us in Passover. Then there is a place for us in Pentecost. Now that we have walked and run with the Lord in these first two Feasts, we understand that He will meet with us yet a third time in Tabernacles! Mount up and soar, you sons of God! It's time to fly!

> But they that wait upon the Lord shall renew [exchange] their strength; they shall mount up with wings as eagles; they shall run, and not be weary; and they shall walk, and not faint (Isaiah 40:31).

THE CHARACTERISTICS OF THE PSALMS OF ASCENT

The *Ascending Offering* (the Burnt Offering) and the *Psalms of Ascent* (the Songs of Degrees) are powerful Old Testament patterns that help us understand the secrets of the ascended life.

In closing this chapter, we note finally that the 15 Psalms of Ascent can be divided into three grades of advancement concerning our spiritual life. This again illustrates the principle of three-fold things (Prov. 22:20-21). There is a three-fold ascending and a three-fold song as we wind our way upward from Passover (thanksgiving) into Pentecost (praise) and then higher still into Tabernacles (worship).

First, Psalms 120-124 is for the *beginners*. There is constant reference to trouble and danger. In this 30-fold realm, we need the constant cleansing of the Laver as we move from the earthly to the heavenly.

Note these chapter themes:

Psalm 120 – Deliverance from the confusion of a deceitful tongue; renunciation and separation from Babylon, self, and others.

Psalm 121 – Preservation.

Psalm 122 – Peace within God's habitation.

Psalm 123 – Patience in vision; the Psalm of the Eyes; the Passover lamb.

Psalm 124 – Dependence upon the Lord; consequent thanksgiving.

Second, Psalms 125-129 is for the *progressors*. There is constant reference to a confidence in God. In this 60-fold realm, the candlestick lights our path as we move from that which is soulish to all that is spiritual.

Note these chapter themes:

Psalm 125 – Trust with resultant confidence.

Psalm 126 – Joy in communion.

Psalm 127 – Total commitment of works; the Builder's Psalm.

Psalm 128 – Fear of God and consequent blessing.

Psalm 129 – Victory over affliction.

Third, Psalms 130-134 is for the *perfect (mature)*. There is constant reference to our communion with Him in His house. In this 100-fold realm, we live in the mercy-seat, having ascended from duality to simplicity and singleness.

The highest order of anything is to become that thing. Consummately, we *become* the song.

Note these chapter themes:

Psalm 130 – Waiting for redemption out of the depths.

Psalm 131 – Humility, lowliness, and meekness.

Psalm 132 – Determination motivated by desire.

Psalm 133 – Unity, anointing, and blessing; union with Him.

Psalm 134 – Praise and worship, perfected ministry; the constant blessing of God flowing out of Zion, the place of His habitation.

In all this, there appears to be a paradox, a seeming contradiction. How is it that we have already ascended with Him and are already seated in the Most Holy Place, and yet we are gradually ascending from here to there (through these three levels containing 15 degrees)?

The answer is simple. We can only ascend experientially to the extent that we understand that we have already ascended in Christ. All is based upon His finished work (John 19:30; Heb. 4:3). Our capacity for Him is enlarging.

Now that we know that the ascended life is *His* life, and that this Kingdom truth about the ascended life is both rich and vast in its Old Testament typology, it is time to acknowledge, appropriate, and manifest His nature and ministry.

The following four chapters compose the heart of this manuscript. We are about to explore the secret, the perspective, the impartation, and the application of the ascended life.

The next chapter is perhaps the most important and pivotal of all. We will never express the life of the Ascended One until we discover its *secret*.

ENDNOTES

1. James Strong. *Strong's Dictionary of Bible Words* (New York, New York: Nelson Reference, 1996), #4609.

2. Ibid., #4608.

3. Fifteen is the biblical number denoting *rest* (see Lev. 23:5-7,34-35,39; Num. 28:17-19; 29:12; 2 Kings 20:6: Esther 9:18-21; Isa. 38:5; Luke 3:1-6; and Gal. 1:18).

4. One of the chapters in my book, *Prevail: A Handbook for the Overcomer*, is given this title. It is an in-depth look at the truth that our salvation is progressive, and clearly explains the transformation of the soul and the renewing of the mind.

5. Apostle G.C. McCurry, one of my mentors, is still active in ministry. He can be contacted at P.O. Box 135, Arnoldsville, GA 30619. Phone 706-742-7701.

Chapter Four

THE ASCENDED LIFE: ITS SECRET

The way of life winds upward for the wise, that he may turn away from hell below (Proverbs 15:24, NKJV).

Life ascends to the heights for the thoughtful—it's a clean about-face from descent into hell (Proverbs 15:24, The Message Bible).

Jesus is the Way of life (John 14:6). The ascended life is *His* life. In the previous two chapters, we have seen this pictured for us in the Old Testament by the *Ascending Offering* and the *Psalms of Ascent.*

Now we come to the heart of the matter. Chapters Four through Seven comprise the focal point of this message. We are about to examine the secret, the perspective, the impartation, and the application of the ascended life.

THE SECRET OF THE ASCENDED LIFE

But he who unites himself with the Lord is one with Him in spirit (1 Corinthians 6:17, NIV).

The *secret* of the ascended life is the Spirit-revealed awareness, the living understanding of our *union* with Him, the Ascended One, in the Most Holy Place!

This is not something we try to do. It is not something that we attain in our own wisdom or strength—it is something that just is!

We do not have to strain or strive for this. This savor of Christ is totally unlike the sweat of Adam. You can make a mistake and still have this. You can mess up this week and not lose this. The "eternal Spirit" (Heb. 9:14) will reveal to you these eternal secrets.

Howbeit when He, the Spirit of truth, is come, He will guide [show the way] *you into all truth...* (John 16:13). Compare Romans 8:14.

God's true sons are guided and led by His Spirit. Only He can show us that the lesser realms beneath are marked by duality, where men and women think in terms of *two*. There in the Feasts of Passover and Pentecost, the emphasis is upon Jesus *and* the devil, upon Christ (the new man) *and* Adam (the old man), upon male *and* female, upon black *and* white.

In the Most Holy Place, the Feast of Tabernacles, our focus, emphasis, and vision is upon Jesus and the Christ (the new man). Here, in the ascended place, we transcend all gender and racial prejudice (Gal. 3:26-28)!

THE SECRET COUNCIL

This *secret* of the ascended life, that we are in union with the ascended One, is revealed by two Hebrew words.

The first describes a secret or private council, a family circle in which secrets are shared. It carries the ideas of fellowship and counsel. The other word speaks about our covering and protection. The first word has to do with our fellowship *with* Christ. The second has to do with our safety *in* Christ.

First, the Hebrew word translated as "secret" or "counsel" in the five references given below is *sode*[1], and it means, "a session, a company of persons (in close deliberation); by implication, intimacy, consultation; council (familiar conversations), divan, circle (familiar friends), intimacy with God (familiar converse)." Its root means, "to sit down together."

*Hast thou heard the **secret** of God?...* (Job 15:8, Emphasis added).

Do you listen in on God's council?... (Job 15:8, NIV)

You who are about to graduate from high school or college, have you heard the secret of God? You love to listen to your favorite music on your MP3 player or iPod[2], but have you ever listened in to the sound of God's council? You who will be parents for the first time in the next five years, are you aware of this privileged mystery?

*As I was in the days of my youth, when the **secret** of God was upon my tabernacle;*

When the Almighty was yet with me, when my children were about me;

When I washed my steps with butter, and the rock poured me out rivers of oil; (Job 29:4-6, Emphasis added).

69

Have you ever sat down and talked together with God? Have you heard the secret of God? Has He ever invited you into His circle? Is the secret of God upon your tabernacle, your life?

> The **secret** *of the Lord is with them that fear Him; and He will show them His covenant* (Psalm 25:14, Emphasis added).

Do you fear and reverence the Lord? Have you ever been intimate with God and He with you? Did you speak with Him this morning? Only those who fear Him will sit down and talk with Him.

> *For who hath stood in the* **counsel** *of the Lord, and hath perceived and heard His word?...* (Jeremiah 23:18, Emphasis added).

To understand the Bible, you must spend time with the Author. I would like to ask every preacher on the planet this question: Have you "perceived" (seen) His Word?

> *Surely the Lord God will do nothing, but He revealeth His* **secret** *unto His servants the prophets* (Amos 3:7, Emphasis added).

Real prophets live in the inner sanctuary. We listen more than we speak. When we speak, we speak the words of Him who sent us, nothing more, nothing less (John 3:34; 14:24; 20:21).

It troubles me that so many immature Christians and insecure preachers think, "If I could just get to know this famous person, or if I could just break into that inner circle of influence...." Even famous people are mere people. But have you been introduced to *Him*? Would you like to fellowship in *His* circle? Have you ever met with God in His secret place?

Because of Jesus' shed blood, we can sit down at His table and talk with Him, face to face.[3]

> *Having therefore, brethren, boldness to enter into the holiest by the blood of Jesus,*
>
> *By a new* [freshly slain] *and living way, which He hath consecrated for us, through the veil, that is to say, His flesh;*
>
> *And having an high priest over the house of God;*
>
> *Let us draw near with a true heart in full assurance of faith…*(Hebrews 10:19-22).

The ascended life begins at our new birth, when we are "born again," literally, "born from above" (John 3:7). From that moment, every child of God is privileged by the blood of Jesus to boldly enter the holiest of all. His grace permits the youngest Christian to go in, sit down in His divine presence, be still, and then listen to God talk to Himself!

The grandest truth of the New Covenant in His blood is the rent veil. Now you can hear His voice in your spirit. The door is open (Rev. 4:1). He tore the curtain. Come in and sit down together with God. Your ears are about to hear privileged information.

This high calling, this ascended life, is not deep and mysterious. It is not a spiritual Never-Neverland. In the place far above, you convene with God. As with intimate friends, both talk and both listen. The ascended life is the life of hearing His voice. The secret of this lifestyle is the sweet hour of prayer.

> *That which we have seen and heard declare we unto you, that ye also may have fellowship with us: and truly our*

fellowship is with the Father, and with His Son Jesus Christ (1 John 1:3).

Intertheistically, the Godhead—the Father, the Son, and the Holy Spirit—sit in secret council. Have you ever heard Them talk to themselves about you? You are the apple of Their eye (Deut. 32:10; Ps.17:8). You are on Their mind all the time—God has a mind full of man (Ps. 8:4).

Within the inner circle of Himself, God took counsel with Himself about you before you were born.[4] The Godhead deliberated and consulted together concerning your destiny. Their purposed will has predetermined the greatness of your life. Do you have any idea what They talked about? Have you heard that secret? Now, because of His blood, you can go right into the planning chambers! The secret of the ascended life is our union with the ascended One who is our life.

Are you bored? Don't know what to do with your time? I know why. You've never heard His secret, His plans and envisioned purpose for His glorious Church.

But he that is joined [glued, cemented, fastened; to cleave] *unto the Lord is one spirit* (1 Corinthians 6:17).

For we are members of His body, of His flesh, and of His bones.

For this cause shall a man leave his father and mother, and shall be joined unto his wife, and they two shall be one flesh.

This is a great mystery: but I speak concerning Christ and the church (Ephesians 5:30-32).

As with married love, we are joined to the Lord in covenantal union. There are some things you never learned about your beloved until you were married. That was privileged information that you didn't know until you became one with him or (her). In marriage, there is an intimacy, confidentiality, and a holiness; something happens within the marriage covenant that is so precious.

Is there a call of God on your life? Have you gone into the secret chambers, cried puddles of tears, and said, "Oh, God, open to me Your mysteries"?

I remember a young man who was saved at the age of 17, then filled with the Holy Ghost and called to the ministry at 19. But I really didn't learn about God until I met those men and women who lived with God in a higher dimension. When they talked, they talked out of a different place. Those encounters with real apostles and prophets, male and female, changed my life.

The most prized thing I have ever encountered while breathing is to sit in the King's council and listen to God talk to Himself. In 1979, the year our oldest daughter, April, was born, the heavens opened and I saw the throne room (Rev. 4). I envisioned the mercy-seat. Ever since, I have maintained a conscious knowing that I am seated with Him in heavenly places. Even in moments of duress and temptation, I am deeply aware of my sharing His ascended life. I am speaking and writing to you *now* out of that.

Have you heard the voice of God? Have you heard His secret?

Behold God's head. Behold His wisdom—He is too wise to make a mistake. He made you, and you are not a mistake.

Behold His hand. Behold His power—He is too powerful to fail. And then behold His heart. Behold His love—He loves you too much to hurt you.

I call to remembrance my song in the night: I commune with mine own heart: and my spirit made diligent search (Psalm 77:6).

As I travel throughout this country and the nations, many times even if there is no one around to talk with spiritually, I talk to myself and commune with my own heart. Sometimes when I get discouraged, I will play one of my own tapes or read one of my own books to encourage myself (1 Sam. 30:6).

God sits in the secret chambers and talks with Himself. He does that until somebody joins Him. He is in session now. Won't you come in? The door is open…

THE SECRET PLACE OF THE MOST HIGH

The secret of the ascended life is consciously knowing that you are one with Him, and have the legal right to sit down with Him in His private council.

The first word for "secret" had to do with our fellowship *with* Christ. The other has to do with our safety *in* Christ.

The second Hebrew word for "secret" speaks about a secret place, a hiding place, and covert. It is *say'-ther*[5], and it means, "a cover; a covering, a shelter, a hiding place, secrecy; protection." This is the Most Holy Place, the secret place of the Most High. Consider these usages, emphasis added:

For in the time of trouble He shall hide me in His pavilion: in the secret of His tabernacle shall He hide me; He shall set me up upon a rock (Psalm 27:5).

74

*Thou shalt hide them in the **secret** of Thy presence from the pride of man: Thou shalt keep them secretly in a pavilion from the strife of tongues* (Psalm 31:20).

*Thou art my **hiding place**; Thou shalt preserve me from trouble; Thou shalt compass me about with songs of deliverance. Selah* (Psalm 32:7).

*I will abide in Thy tabernacle for ever: I will trust in the **covert** of Thy wings. Selah* (Psalm 61:4).

*Thou calledst in trouble, and I delivered thee; I answered thee in the **secret place** of thunder...* (Psalm 81:7).

*He that dwelleth in the **secret place** of the most High shall abide under the shadow of the Almighty* (Psalm 91:1).

*Thou art my **hiding place** and my shield: I hope in Thy word* (Psalm 119:114).

Again, the first Hebrew word and set of scriptures described our fellowship *with* Christ. This second word and set of scriptures just expressed the safety of our being *in* Christ!

The *secret* of the ascended life is our union with Him in the Most Holy Place. The ascended life is *His* life.

When He ascended, we ascended. Now we are ready for a new *perspective*, to see everyone and everything through the eyes of God!

ENDNOTES

1. James Strong. *Strong's Dictionary of Bible Words* (New York, New York: Nelson Reference, 1996), #5475.

2. The iPod is a product of the Apple Corporation.

3. The patriarch Jacob (Gen. 32:30), the shepherd Moses (Ex. 33:22; Num. 14:14, Deut. 5:4; 34:10), the cowardly judge Gideon (Judg. 6:22), and the nation of Israel in the wilderness (Ezek. 30:35) all saw God "face to face." Note as well that this is promised to believers (1 Cor. 13:12).

4. This truth is unfolded in-depth in my book, *Chosen for Greatness*. We were chosen out of the Word, the *Logos*, before we were born (Eph. 1:4). Each of us is a *rhema* word from God, sent here to this planet on assignment. This is His will, plan, and purpose, and our destiny.

5. Strong, #5643.

Chapter Five

THE ASCENDED LIFE: ITS PERSPECTIVE

The previous chapter shared the *secret* of the ascended life: our union with the ascended One who sits enthroned between the wings of the cherubim in the Most Holy Place.

...he [Moses] *endured, as seeing Him who is invisible* (Hebrews 11:27).

Once we receive this revelatory insight that we have risen and ascended with Him, we immediately begin to see everything and everyone differently—the ascended life brings to us a new *perspective*! These new eyes for the invisible present another whole new set of values—God's point of view, His outlook, standpoint, and angle. Everything about the scene and picture changes.

Now we look through the eyes of God!

We must see God before we can effectively speak His Word, communicating what we have seen by the Spirit.

This revealed Word impacts men and women, lifting them into new dimensions. We rub the salve of God upon their eyes (Rev. 3:18). We equip them to see things that they have never understood before, and bring them into a new understanding about themselves and their role in His ultimate purpose, and how that purpose unfolds. We adjust their worldview to line up with the Word of God.

> *But Jonathan heard not when his father charged the people with the oath: wherefore he put forth the end of the rod that was in his hand, and dipped it in an honeycomb, and put his hand to his mouth; and his eyes were enlightened* (1 Samuel 14:27).

> *The eyes of your understanding* [heart] *being enlightened; that ye may know what is the hope of His calling...* (Ephesians 1:18).

To see is to understand. Like Jonathan of old, we have tasted the sweet honey of God's Word. As He did with Cleophas and his young friend on the way to Emmaus, Jesus has opened our minds and hearts that we might understand the Scriptures (Luke 24:45).

FROM WHENCE WE LOOK

> *In the year that king Uzziah died I saw also the Lord sitting upon a throne, high and lifted up, and His train* [the skirt of a robe] *filled the temple* (Isaiah 6:1).

The prophet Isaiah received an upward, an inward, and then an outward vision (Isa. 6:1-8). Once He saw the Lord *high and lifted up,* he saw himself and then his world. Our worldview, our whole value system, how we compute, hinges upon our *perspective.* We are partakers of the ascended life. The higher we go, the further we can see!

How do you see God? And how does God see?

For our conversation is in heaven; from whence [which] also we look for the Saviour, the Lord Jesus Christ: (Philippians 3:20).

Our citizenship is in heaven....(NIV, NKJV)

But we are citizens of the state (commonwealth, homeland) which is in heaven....(AMP)

The word "conversation" here is *politeuma*[1], and it means, "a community; citizenship, a state or commonwealth of citizens." It is derived from the verb *politeuomai* (to behave as a citizen; to conduct oneself as pledged to some law of life). We are not citizens of earth. We are citizens of Heaven in the earth. We are citizens of His commonwealth; we have some wealth in common (Rom. 8:17; Eph. 2:12; 1 Pet. 3:7).

Paul was a Roman citizen and Philippi was a colony in the Roman province of Macedonia. Acts 16 is the backdrop to Philippians. The apostle uses this word *politeuma* to show us that our manner of life is in the heavenly places. It is from that posture that we "look."

For the law of the Spirit of life in Christ Jesus hath made me free from the law of sin and death (Romans 8:2).

Our citizenry, all our rights and privileges, are in the heavens. This ascended life is the higher life. We cannot behave as citizens of Heaven until we see what God sees, how God sees, and when God sees. We regulate and conduct our lives according to the "royal law," the "law of liberty"

(James 1:25; 2:8,12). Heaven's law is the "law of faith" (Rom. 3:27), the "law of God after the inward man" (Rom. 7:22), the "law of righteousness" (Rom. 9:31), and the "law of Christ" (Gal. 6:2). The law of His new nature dictates from *within* innately and intuitively by the Spirit *how* we see and *what* we see.

There is a new nature in us that has made a pledge and a vow with the law of the Spirit of life in Christ Jesus.

Those who cannot see through the eyes of God have yet to ascend. America's churches are filled with folks who may or may not be saved, born from above. Justification gives us a new standing, and regeneration gives us a new heart.

The new birth is not just a birth. It is a quickening as we pass from death unto life (Eph. 2:1; 1 John 3:14). It is a resurrection (Rom. 6:3-5). It is a creation (2 Cor. 5:17). Once we have been born from above, we are raised up with Him. We have arisen to walk in newness of life. This walk, this conversation, this citizenship is in the heavens.

And He [Jesus] *said unto them, Ye are from beneath; I am from above: ye are of this world; I am not of this world* (John 8:23).

In a previous chapter, we contrasted that which is from "above" with that which is from "beneath." Christ is above and Adam is beneath. Our perspective, our point of view, is from above. In Christ, nothing is above us. Everything else— that which is outside of Christ—is beneath us, and is a lying vanity. My Christian friend, there is nothing that can get on top of you!

COME UP

The invitation is out: "Come up!" We have been commanded to "come up" unto the Lord into this new perspective. We have come up positionally, but we need to arise experientially into this new perspective. We need to come up into the expression and manifestation of it. Note these key passages where God's people were commanded to "come up" unto the Lord.

*And He said unto Moses, **come up** unto the Lord, thou, and Aaron, Nadab, and Abihu, and seventy of the elders of Israel; and worship ye afar off* (Exodus 24:1, Emphasis added). Compare Exodus 24:12.

The first time Moses went to the top of the mountain, he was commanded to "come up" by himself (Ex. 19:1-23). Now he is to bring his family, his brother and his nephews. Have you ascended, Mom? Have you come up, Dad? Have you brought your family? Have you brought the kids? It is noble and right that you have given them a good education, but have you shown them how to pray, how to ascend the mountain of God?

Those of us who make up the Joshua generation have a great responsibility and stewardship. Our purpose is to cause others to inherit. We have ascended. Now it is time to take the rest of family up to see God.

*And be ready in the morning, and **come up** in the morning unto mount Sinai, and present thyself there to Me in the top of the mount* (Exodus 34:2, Emphasis added).

The life of Moses exemplifies the ascended life. Be ready to ascend in the morning of this new day. The glorious

Church will be presented to the Lord without spot or wrinkle (Eph. 5:25-27).

> *Put not forth thyself in the presence of the king, and stand not in the place of great men:*
>
> *For better it is that it be said unto thee, **come up** hither...*(Proverbs 25:6-7, Emphasis added).

Each of us has been invited to come into the King's presence.

We have been invited by the King Himself to share His secret chambers. Like Mephibosheth of old, we are now blessed to sit at the King's table for the rest of our lives (2 Sam. 9). Come and dine. Our worldview has changed. Another secret of the ascended life is that now we can see everyone and everything through the eyes of God!

> *And saviours* [deliverers] *shall **come up** on Mount Zion to judge the mount of Esau; and the Kingdom shall be the Lord's* (Obadiah 21, Emphasis added).

The corporate Overcomer of the end-times shall come up on Mount Zion and judge the mount of Esau, the flesh. We are not qualified to assess anything until we have ascended to receive His point of view. Everything must be adjudicated through the eyes of our pure and righteous God. In and of ourselves, we cannot distinguish or discriminate, separating the precious from the vile (Jer. 15:19), the lower realms. Otherwise we will judge someone or something after the limited vision of the flesh and not after the Spirit (2 Cor. 5:16-17).

Now apply this truth to the local church family. If we were to view everyone in Christ, there would never be any grumbling, unbelief, procrastination, or competition.

Have you seen your husband the way that God sees him? Do you look at your wife through the eyes of the Spirit? How do you see your children?

> *After this I looked, and, behold, a door was opened in heaven: and the first voice which I heard was as it were of a trumpet talking with me; which said, **Come up** hither, and I will show thee things which must be hereafter* (Revelation 4:1, Emphasis added).

The throne room, the Most Holy Place, is a present reality. The open door of this latter verse vividly pictures the rent veil. Everything that had been hidden for ages and generations is now made manifest to the saints of God (Col. 1:26). Come up!

A NEW PERSPECTIVE OF OUR FEARS

The secret of the ascended life is our union with the ascended One. Once we receive this revelatory insight that we have ascended with Him, we immediately receive a new *perspective*! This new point of view manifests in two primary areas, with regard to:

1. Our *fears*, our enemies.

2. His *favor*, His blessings.

You don't have to wait until tomorrow to walk in this. The prophetic anointing and the word of faith within these pages will enable you to immediately participate in this new point of view!

First, the ascended life brings to us a new viewpoint of our *fears*, our enemies. We have no adversaries but fear itself. Once we move up into the ascended posture, we look at our enemies through the eyes of God. This is illustrated in a familiar Old Testament story.

And the Lord spake unto Moses, saying,

Send thou men, that they may search the land of Canaan, which I give unto the children of Israel: of every tribe of their fathers shall ye send a man, every one a ruler among them (Numbers 13:1-2).

These were not children who were sent to explore the new land. Each of the 12 spies was a mature man and a ruler. These were not ordinary folks. This word for *ruler* means, "an exalted one; a king or a sheik; a captain, chief, governor, prince, or leader." The Septuagint uses a Greek word which means, "a ruler, lord, prince, authority, or official."

These 12 men who represented each of the tribes were men of great authority.

And they returned from searching of the land after forty days [the biblical number for trial and testing].

And they went and came to Moses, and to Aaron, and to all the congregation of the children of Israel, unto the wilderness of Paran, to Kadesh; and brought back word unto them, and unto all the congregation, and showed them the fruit of the land.

And they told him, and said, We came unto the land whither thou sentest us, and surely it floweth with milk and honey; and this is the fruit of it (Numbers 13:25-27).

The spies brought back more than a word or message about the land. They actually produced the "fruit" or the evidence of it! They brought back the grapes of Eshcol, which means, "cluster" (Num. 13:23-24). They said, "God's Word is true. This place is real. Surely the land flows with milk and honey."

Nevertheless the people be strong [harsh, fierce] *that dwell in the land, and the cities are walled, and very great: and moreover we saw the children of Anak there.*

The Amalekites dwell in the land of the south: and the Hittites, and the Jebusites, and the Amorites, dwell in the mountains: and the Canaanites dwell by the sea, and by the coast of Jordan (Numbers 13:28-29).

"Nevertheless," the ten continued, "we *saw* the children of Anak (a race of giants)." Note their perspective. They were looking at their enemies from the lower, earthy, human, or natural point of view. How do you see and deal with the sons of Anak, your circumstances? If you look at situations from beneath, they will take your breath away, and you will give up. It will take you down. You will quit.

And Caleb stilled the people before Moses, and said, Let us go up at once, and possess it; for we are well able to overcome it (Number 13:30).

In the Hebrew, this is an interjection. Caleb said, "Hush! Keep silence! Be silent! Hold (one's) peace! Hold (one's) tongue! Be still!" This man was a real leader who saw the *same* giants and walled cities from another perspective! This overcomer knew that they were to "go up" (ascend) at once and possess the promise, that they were well able to "overcome" (to prevail, to gain or accomplish, to be able to reach). Beloved, we've got the firstfruits, the earnest (Num. 13:20 with Rom. 8:23; Eph. 1:13-14). The rest is on the way!

Folks who have not ascended view their enemies from beneath. They just won't be still, going on and on about their circumstances. Sometimes tough love has to say, "My ears are not slop buckets. I don't want to hear that any more. Stop talking about it." Stop listening to your adversary. You can always tell when the devil is lying to you—his lips are moving! He is the father of lies (John 8:44). It is impossible for God to lie (Heb. 6:18), and it is impossible for satan to tell the truth.

Trust the Lord. Living by faith is not risky because it is based upon the Word of God (Rom. 10:17). We must arise into the ascended life to hear God talk with Himself. In that high place, there is nothing to fear. From that perspective, all our enemies are beneath, defeated, under our feet (Rom. 16:20).

> But the men that went up with him said, We be not able to go up against the people; for they are stronger than we.
>
> And they brought up an evil report of the land which they had searched unto the children of Israel, saying, The land, through which we have gone to search it, is a land that eateth up the inhabitants thereof; and all the people that we saw in it are men of a great stature.
>
> And there we saw the giants, the sons of Anak, which come of the giants: and we were in our own sight [eye] as grasshoppers, and so we were in their sight (Numbers 13:31-33).

This "evil report" literally means, "to move slowly, be sluggish."[2] What really brought fear to the ten unbelieving spies was the possibility of inhabiting a land and realm of "great stature" (Eph. 4:13).

The ascended life brings a new perspective of our fears, our enemies. The verse above (Num. 13:33) is the key to the whole story, for how we see our adversaries determines the strength of our enemy. The adversary's level of attack will be on the basis of how you "see" yourself—"*and so we were in their sight."*

> *And all the congregation lifted up their voice, and cried; and the people wept* [bewail, cry] *that night.*
>
> *And all the children of Israel murmured* [complain, grumble] *against Moses and against Aaron: and the whole congregation said unto them, Would God that we had died in the land of Egypt! or would God we had died in this wilderness!* (Numbers 14:1-2).
>
> [Caleb is speaking] *Only rebel not ye against the Lord, neither fear ye the people of the land; for they are bread for us: their defence* [shade, as a protection] *is departed from them, and the Lord is with us: fear them not* (Numbers 14:9).

The Scriptures reveal two ways to deal with a giant. Like David (1 Sam. 17), we can knock him down and cut off his head (the Word went ahead of the rock), or we can eat him! Using the metaphor of bending over and harvesting by hand, Caleb declared, "They are bread for us!" The key to his heavenly perspective was his awareness that, "The Lord is with us." What about the circumstances of life's situations? "Fear them not!"

Similarly, the prophet Ezekiel sat by the same river in the same land of exile with his fellow captives. While they looked around, moaning and sorrowing, he looked up and saw visions of God (Ps. 137:1-4 with Ezek. 1:1).

But all the congregation bade stone them with stones. And the glory of the Lord appeared in the tabernacle of the congregation before all the children of Israel.

And the Lord said unto Moses, How long will this people provoke [scorn, spurn] Me? and how long will it be ere they believe Me, for all the signs which I have shown among them? (Numbers 14:10-11).

This story provides the historical backdrop to Hebrews 3-4, the passage that exhorts us to enter into His Sabbath rest. We are living in the Seventh Day from Adam (Jude 1:14) and the Third Day from Jesus (Hos. 6:1-3)—the ascended life is the life of rest!

Because all those men which have seen My glory, and My miracles, which I did in Egypt and in the wilderness, and have tempted [try, test] Me now these ten times, and have not hearkened [to listen, obey] to My voice;

Surely they shall not see the land which I sware unto their fathers, neither shall any of them that provoked Me see it:

But My servant Caleb, because he had another spirit with him, and hath followed [after] Me fully, him will I bring into the land whereinto he went; and his seed shall possess it (Numbers 14:22-24).

Because of Israel's stubborn defiance of Caleb's admonition, they were left to wander in the wilderness (with 100 funerals a day for 40 years). They would never "see" (perceive, discern, have vision of) the "land." The New Testament "land," found in the epistle to the Ephesians, is the "land" of heavenly places, the ascended life, the Christ-life (Eph. 1:3; 2:6).

But Caleb had "another spirit," another perspective, another point of view of the *same* giants, walled cities, and all the "ites," all the enemies. Because he fully, wholly followed the Lord (into the ascended life), he *and* his seed were blessed (Josh. 14)! Parents, do this for your children and your children's children.

There is in the earth an end-time company of overcomers who have another spirit, another *perspective*. There is a generation who will not let anything get them down. These prevailers are up against insurmountable odds—the pressures of job and family, betrayal, lies, thievery—yet are so resilient that nothing can stop them! Like Caleb of old, they are determined to receive their inheritance (Josh. 14:12). These find their faith and strength from above in the secret places of God. These have heard the Creator talk with Himself, and there is no defeat in His voice.

These look through the eyes of God. We have been given a new perspective concerning our enemies. We have nothing to fear.

Thou wilt keep him in perfect peace, whose mind is stayed on Thee: because he trusteth in Thee (Isaiah 26:3).

But now thus saith the Lord that created thee, O Jacob, and He that formed thee, O Israel, Fear not: for I have redeemed thee, I have called thee by thy name; thou art Mine.

When thou passest through the waters, I will be with thee; and through the rivers, they shall not overflow thee: when thou walkest through the fire, thou shalt not be burned; neither shall the flame kindle upon thee (Isaiah 43:1-2).

For God hath not given us the spirit of fear [timidity, cowardice]; *but of power* [dunamis], *and of love* [agape], *and of a sound* [disciplined, self-controlled] *mind* (2 Timothy 1:7).

A NEW PERSPECTIVE OF HIS FAVOR

Our enemies are from beneath. His blessings are from above. The ascended life also brings us a fresh perspective of His *favor*, His blessings.

[The King is speaking] *Until the day break, and the shadows flee away, I will get Me to the mountain of myrrh, and to the hill of frankincense. Thou art all fair, My love; there is no spot in thee.* (Song of Solomon 4:6-7).

The "mountain of myrrh" bespeaks His death at Calvary. We have been crucified with Him. The "hill of frankincense" represents His resurrection. He was raised from the dead and accepted by the Father. Because of Christ's finished work, the Shulamite Bride is "fair" (beautiful and bright). There is no "spot," no "stain, blemish, or defect" in her. She has been delivered from the consciousness of sin.

Come with me from Lebanon, my spouse, with me from Lebanon: look from the top of Amana, from the top of Shenir and Hermon, from the lions' dens, from the mountains of the leopards.

Thou hast ravished My heart, My sister, My spouse; thou hast ravished My heart with one of thine eyes, with one chain of thy neck (Song of Solomon 4:8-9).

Here is the invitation of the Bridegroom to ascend—
"Come with me." We are heirs of God, and joint-heirs with
Christ (Rom. 8:17). As with a husband and His wife, we are
heirs together with Him of the grace of life (1 Pet. 3:7).

> *God...hath in these last days spoken unto us by His Son,*
> *whom He hath appointed heir of all things...*(Hebrews
> 1:1-2).

Jesus Christ is the legal, covenantal Heir of "all things"
in Heaven, in earth, and under the earth. We are joint-heirs of
all that He is, all that He has, and all that He does. Paul
declared to the church at Corinth, "...*all things are yours*"
(1 Cor. 3:21). Jesus Christ, our heavenly Husband and Lord,
has "*given unto us all things that pertain unto life and godliness*"
(2 Pet. 1:3; compare Rom. 8:32).

> *For the Lord God is a sun and shield: the Lord will give*
> *grace and glory: no good thing will He withhold from*
> *them that walk uprightly* (Psalm 84:11).

The Bride is commanded to look from the "top" of the
mountain. This is the Hebrew word *ro'sh*, and means, "head;
the top, the summit, the upper part, the chief, the total, the
sum, the height, the front, the beginning." She has ascended
with Him and has grown up into the place of looking from
the posture of His headship (Eph. 1:20-23; 4:15).

> *Blessed be the God and Father of our Lord Jesus Christ,*
> *who hath blessed us with all spiritual blessings in heav-*
> *enly places in Christ* (Ephesians 1:3).

This word for *look* in Song of Solomon 4:8 means, "to
walk around, inspect, spy out, survey; behold, observe,
regard, or watch." His blessings are from above. In every
direction, there are spiritual blessings in heavenly places!

Having surveyed the limitless wealth of her Bridegroom Lover, she asks as she contemplates His splendor, "Is all this Yours?" He smiles as He replies, "All that you see is *ours*." If we can *see* it, we can have it!

> *For all the promises of God in Him are yea, and in Him*
> *Amen, unto the glory of God by us* (2 Corinthians 1:20).

Now note especially the name of this mountain. "Amana" is the English transliteration of the Hebrew word *am-aw-naw'*, which means, "something fixed, covenant, allowance, certain or sure portion." It is used of a covenant or of financial support. It is further derived from *aw-mane'* (sure, faithfulness, truly; Amen! So be it!), from which we get the English, "amen." The root is *aw-man'*, the Hebrew word for "faith."

Amana, the mountain of faith, is named "Amen" or "So be it!" Look from the place of His headship. The eyes are in the Head. You will be certain and sure as you look with His steady perspective. She asked, "Can I have that?" He replies, "Yes!" She can only say, "Amen!"

Moreover, "Shenir" (snow mountain) is the Amorite name for "Hermon" (sanctuary). Interestingly, some have considered the latter to be the ancient Mount of Transfiguration, or the ancient name for Zion. Accordingly, the mountain of blessing and favor is the mountain of change, the mountain of dominion.

Having embraced His love, she has "ravished" His heart and made it beat faster. The New International Version translates Song of Solomon 4:9, *"You have stolen my heart with one glance of your eyes."* Her vision, her perspective is "one." She is single-eyed, marked by the "simplicity" that is in Christ.[3]

This describes the perspective of the ascended life, looking through the eyes of God.

The ascended life in the heavenly places gives us a new perspective of all His *favor*, His blessings. Concerning His promises, He says, "yes" and we say, "amen." This is the revelation of all that we have received through the New Covenant in His blood! With the fearlessness of the "lion" and the speed of the "leopard," we believe God! Lord, we receive Your favor and Your blessing! Amen! So be it!

Blessed be the Lord, who daily loadeth us with benefits, even the God of our salvation. Selah. (Psalm 68:19).

We have ascended, we have stepped up to the top of the mountain. There, we are "loaded" with His benefits and blessings. Now we are ready to descend, to step down, to download and *impart* all that we have received from His hand.

ENDNOTES

1. James Strong. *Strong's Dictionary of Bible Words* (New York, New York: Nelson Reference, 1996), #4175.

2. The "evil report" means "to move slowly, be sluggish." Note these verses in Proverbs about the "sluggard" or "lazy, indolent, slothful" (Prov. 6:6,9; 10:26; 13:4; 26:16).

3. The Glorious Church has a "single" eye (Matt. 6:22; Luke 11:34), the key to life and immortality. In Song of Solomon 4:9, the Bride of Christ lives in the upper realms of His "simplicity." The Greek word is *haplotes* (Strong #572), and it means, "singleness, (subjectively) sincerity (without dissimulation or self-seeking), or (objectively) generosity (copious bestowal); the virtue of one who is free from pretence and hypocrisy" (Rom. 12:8; 2 Cor. 1:12; 11:2-3).

Chapter Six

THE ASCENDED LIFE: ITS IMPARTATION

We are learning the secrets of the ascended life. We have begun to look through the eyes of God. The ascended life is *His* life! Our union with Him in the heavenly places is manifested through the ascended life that flows out of Him. This is expressed in our daily walk by our love for one another. This is the key to our living the high calling.

> *But he who unites himself with the Lord is one with Him in spirit* (1 Corinthians 6:17, NIV).

> *For our conversation* [citizenship] *is in heaven; from whence also we look...*(Philippians 3:20).

We now understand the *secret* that we have ascended with Him, that we are one with Him. In this Most Holy Place, we have received a fresh, new *perspective* and view of everything and everyone.

SOMEBODY NEEDS HELP
AT THE BOTTOM OF THE MOUNTAIN

...as He is, so are we in this world (1 John 4:17).

The *secret* of the ascended life is the revelation that we are one in and with Him, the One who has already ascended. We are seated together with Him in the heavenlies in His throne, the place and seat of all authority (Eph. 2:6; Rev. 3:21). We now can see everything through *His* eyes.

A garden inclosed is my sister, my spouse; a spring shut up, a fountain sealed.

Thy plants are an orchard of pomegranates, with pleasant fruits; camphire, with spikenard,

Spikenard and saffron; calamus and cinnamon, with all trees of frankincense; myrrh and aloes, with all the chief spices: (Song of Solomon 4:12-14).

The fruit of the Spirit is His divine nature (Gal. 5:22-24). With the exception of the pomegranate (which was native to Palestine), all the other eight fruits in the Shulamite's garden had to be imported from another country. We have His Spirit. There is a nature in us now that is out of this world!

So from now on we regard no one from a worldly point of view. Though we once regarded Christ in this way, we do so no longer.

Therefore, if anyone is in Christ, he is a new creation; the old has gone, the new has come! (2 Corinthians 5:16-17, NIV).

The *perspective* of the ascended life immediately gives to us a fresh view of our fears, our enemies. They are beneath us, and we are above them. Moreover, the higher we go, the further we can see His favor, His blessings.

Once we have received from Him, we can begin to download or minister His life to others from the Heavens. The *impartation* of the ascended life is that in Jesus' name we give away and share the *gift* that we *are* and the *gifts* that we *have*!

> *Religion that God our Father accepts as pure and fault-less is this: to look after orphans and widows in their distress and to keep oneself from being polluted by the world* (James 1:27, NIV).

The quiet, meditative, inward Christ-life must become inevitably associated with its active expression in world affairs, especially to the poor and the marginalized of society. Our gospel must break out of the four walls of our churches and reach out into the streets.

We speak out of who we are, not just what we have learned. Before the Word can be powerfully spoken, it must be engrafted and implanted (James 1:21), incarnated into the vessel. Only then can it be effectively reproduced in others.

> *Then answered Peter, and said unto Jesus, Lord, it is good for us to be here: if Thou wilt, let us make here three tabernacles; one for Thee, and one for Moses, and one for Elias* (Matthew 17:4).

On the Mount of Transfiguration, Peter wanted to stay in the ascended place. But it is not good that we stay there. At the bottom of the mountain is a great need.

The besetting historical weakness of classical sonship was a tendency to become spiritual hermits who thrive on the revelatory understanding of the Scriptures. The byword has been, "Are you in the message?" Sadly, this exclusivism has often bred arrogance and spiritual pride. But the world will know us by our fruit (His nature), not our abundance of revelation (2 Cor. 12:7). It is not what we know, but rather Whom we know and Whose we are.

Once we grasp the secret of this high calling and partake of the new global worldview that flows out of that, we must understand the purpose for the ascended life. Why did the Bridegroom invite us to come up and to look from the top?

Peter, James, and John were picked to go up the mountain with Him. James explains the faith of God. Peter's writings tell us the hope of God. John was the one chosen to reveal the love of God. Jesus carried faith, hope, and love to the top of that mountain, to the highest level (1 Cor. 13:13).

But they (and we) cannot stay in that ascended place. Somebody needs help at the bottom of the mountain! None of the preachers in the lower realms could fix this problem; none had the answer to this desperate human situation.

Lord, have mercy on my son: for he is lunatic, and sore vexed: for ofttimes he falleth into the fire, and oft into the water (Matthew 17:15). Compare Matthew 4:24.

This boy was a *lunatic*, which means, "to be moonstruck, crazy." The moon can symbolize the law, or the powers of darkness. Millions in this nation and the nations are bound by legalism and a fear of the devil. Jesus and his friends—faith, hope, and love—had to *descend*, to come down from that ascended place, to meet this need!

We learned in Chapter One that the Greek word for ascend is *anabaino*, and it means, "to walk up, to step up." The word for descend is *katabaino*, which means, "to walk down, to step down." The only reason that God has privileged us to step up into the ascended life is so we can step down from that place and minister to others.

Another picture of this is found in John 8 where the Lord stooped before He spoke (John 8:6). He knelt *down* to minister to the woman taken in adultery. The only ones who are truly qualified to stoop and to serve broken humanity are those who have first ascended. Until we ascend into Him and receive of Him, we have nothing to say and nothing to give.

EVERY GOOD GIFT AND EVERY PERFECT GIFT

We cannot remain in the lofty places and live unto ourselves. We have ascended with Him, and are one with Him. We have received a new perspective of everything and everyone. Now we must begin to *impart* His life and love to others from the Heavens.

Again, the *impartation* of the ascended life is that we give away and share the *gift* that we *are* and the *gifts* that we *have*! He has made you His gift, and He has given you gifts.

Every good gift and every perfect gift is from above, and cometh down from the Father of lights, with whom is no variableness, neither shadow of turning (James 1:17).

Every good and perfect gift is from above, coming down from the Father of the heavenly lights, who does not change like shifting shadows (James 1:17, NIV).

Every good gift and every perfect (free, large, full) gift is from above; it comes down from the Father of all [that gives] light, in [the shining of] Whom there can be no variation [rising from setting] or shadow cast by His turning [as in an eclipse] (James 1:17, AMP).

In Christ, we are both "good" and "perfect" (complete). Like Jesus, we are from "above" and not "beneath" (John 8:23). All the gifts that we have flow out of the gift that we are!

I want to emphasize that *gift* that you *are*, but the following Scriptures tell of the gifts that you *have*.

The Greek word for "gift" or "gifts" in all the verses below is *charisma*[1], and it means, "a (divine) gratuity; (specifically) a (spiritual) endowment, (subjectively) religious qualification, or (objectively) miraculous faculty; a favor with which one receives without any merit of his own; grace or gifts denoting extraordinary powers, distinguishing certain Christians and enabling them to serve the church of Christ." Thayer's Greek Lexicon adds, "a gift of grace, a gift involving grace (*charis*) on the part of God as the donor." These *charismata* are "grace-gifts." Consider these examples, emphasis added:

*For the **gifts** and [the] calling of God are without repentance* (Romans 11:29).

*Having then **gifts** differing [varying in kind] according to the grace that is given to us...*(Romans 12:6).

*Now there are diversities [division, distribution, distinction] of **gifts**, but the same Spirit* (1 Corinthians 12:4).

*Do not neglect your **gift**, which was given you through a prophetic message when the body of elders [presbytery, KJV] laid their hands on you* (1 Timothy 4:14, NIV).

*For this reason I remind you to fan into flame the **gift** of God, which is in you through the laying on of my hands* (2 Timothy 1:6, NIV).

100

*Each one should use whatever **gift** he has received to serve others, faithfully administering God's grace in its various forms* (1 Peter 4:10, NIV).

Each of us is a gift from above, and each of us has been given gifts from above (that flow out of the gift which we are). What we *do* flows out of who we *are* in Christ!

For in Him we live, and move, and have our being... (Acts 17:28).

And whatsoever ye do in word or deed, do all in the name [nature] *of the Lord Jesus, giving thanks to God and the Father by* [through] *Him (Colossians 3:17).*

THE ASCENDED LIFE IS THE LIFE OF IMPARTATION

Once we see with a new perspective, we are ready to be able ministers of the New Covenant, to give away His life to others.

This new life is *His* life. It is the sound and voice of resurrection life that flows out from between the wings of the cherubim in the Most Holy Place. This Christ-life has a distinct fragrance.

As we exegete James 1:17 in the following sections, note these key principles of imparting the ascended life.

Every good gift and every perfect gift...(James 1:17)

The Greek word for "gift" in this verse is *dosis*[2], and it means, "a giving; a gift." *Vine's*[3] adds, "as a matter of debt." We are debtors to love, and the law of love is giving (John 3:16)! *Dosis* is derived from the verb *didomi* (to give, bestow a gift, grant, supply, offer, yield). Consider these usages of the latter, emphasis added:[4]

*John answered and said, A man can receive nothing, except it be **given** him from heaven* (John 3:27).

*For the bread of God is He [Jesus and His Church] which cometh down from heaven, and **giveth** life unto the world* (John 6:33).

*Wherefore he saith, When He ascended up on high, He led captivity captive, and **gave** gifts unto men* (Ephesians 4:8).

These verses describe the source, the attitude, and the spirit in which we are to give ourselves and our gifts away to others! You are somebody's bread. Somebody is feeding on the mention of your name. The very thought of you brings strength to others.

Each of us is a gift that is "good." God is good and in Him we are good. God is perfect and in Him we are perfect. This revelation flows from our ascended perspective.

The Greek word for "good" in James 1:17 is *agathos*[5], and it means, "good (in any sense, often as a noun); of good constitution or nature; useful, salutary; pleasant, agreeable, joyful, happy; excellent, distinguished; upright, honorable."

This word speaks of intrinsic goodness, that which is beneficial in its effect. We constitute the benefits of God to others (*agathos* is translated as "benefit" in Philem. 1:14). You are a walking, talking benefit from the Lord to others. Out from you flows an aura of beneficial goodness.

The Greek word for "perfect" in James 1:17 is *teleios*[6], and it means, "complete (in various applications of labor, growth, mental, and moral character); brought to its end, finished; wanting nothing necessary to completeness; consummate human integrity and virtue." It is used to describe full grown men, adults, and those of full age or mature.

Our gift flows out of His finished work (John 19:30). The "perfect" gift that we are is enough to meet the need. Note the usages of this descriptive adjective regarding our imparting the ascended life to others, emphasis added:[7]

> *Be ye therefore **perfect**, even as your Father which is in heaven is perfect* (Matthew 5:48).

> *Till we all come in the unity of the faith, and of the knowledge of the Son of God, unto a **perfect** man, unto the measure of the stature of the fulness of Christ:* (Ephesians 4:13).

> *Herein is our love made **perfect**, that we may have boldness in the day of judgment: because as He is, so are we in this world.*

> *There is no fear in love; but **perfect** love casteth out fear: because fear hath torment. He that feareth is not made **perfect** in love* (1 John 4:17-18).

The good and perfect gift which we are "is" from above (James 1:17). This word is *eimi*, and it means, "the first person singular present indicative; I exist or I AM; to be, to exist, to happen, to be present." It points to who we *are* in Christ. You don't have to wait for an invitation to impart His ascended life. You just stay on "go." I hear the Lord say, "Be who and what I would be if I were there."

We must not think of ourselves more highly than we ought to think (Rom. 12:3). But we must think of ourselves more lowly than we ought to think. We must see ourselves in Christ.

CELESTIAL BEINGS ARE COMING DOWN TO EARTH

...is from above, and cometh down...(James 1:17)

Every good and perfect gift is "from above" (James 1:17). This word is *anothen*[8], and it means, "from above; by analogy, from the first; by implication, anew; from a higher place; used of things which come from heaven or God; from the first, from the beginning, from the very first; anew, over again." It is derived from *ano* (upward, on the top, above, on high, northward); it flows down out of the ascended life. Consider these keys to impartation that flow "from above."

And, behold, the veil of the temple was rent in twain from the top [from above] *to the bottom...*(Matthew 27:51).

Marvel not that I said unto thee, Ye must be born again [from above] (John 3:7).

But the wisdom that is from above...(James 3:17).

Every good and perfect gift "cometh down" (James 1:17). This is the present, active verb *katabaino*[9], and it means, "to descend, to go down, to come down, to descend." It is used of celestial (heavenly) beings coming down to earth.

Katabaino is a compound of *kata* (down) and *baino* (to walk); the root of the latter is *basis* (step, walk; foot). We are seated (enthroned) with Christ; we have to step down (*kata*) from that throne in grateful humility to serve others. We cannot step down (*katabaino*) until we step up, until we ascend (*anabaino*). As we download and give away His life, we arm and equip the body of Christ to do the work of the ministry (Eph. 4:12). Consider these usages of *katabaino*, emphasis added:

*And as they **came down** from the mountain,* [of Trans-figuration to minister to the lunatic boy]...(Matthew 17:9).

*For the bread of God is he which **cometh down** from heaven, and giveth life unto the world* (John 6:33).

*Be of the same mind one toward another. Mind not high things, but **condescend** to men of low estate. Be not wise in your own conceits* (Romans 12:16).

This word for "condescend" in Romans 12:16 is a different word from *katabaino*, but it conveys the same truth. It means, "to yield to lowly things."

The previous chapter revealed our new perspective of His favor, all His blessings. As joint-heirs of His bounty (Rom. 8:17), we now share His Word and ministry of reconciliation (2 Cor. 5:17-21). We are to bring Heaven to earth. The corporate Overcomer comes down out of the New Jerusalem of Heaven from God (Rev. 3:12).

Thy kingdom come. Thy will be done in earth, as it is in heaven (Matthew 6:10).

THE FATHER OF LIGHTS

...and cometh down from the Father of lights. (James 1:17).

Every good and perfect gift comes down from the "Father of lights." In Hebrews 12:9, He is also called the "father of spirits." The Greek word for "lights" in our text is *phos*[10], and it means, "to shine or make manifest, especially by rays; luminousness; light (emitted by a lamp, or by a star); a lamp or a torch." *Phos* is also rendered in the King James Version as "fire."

Ye are the light of the world...(Matthew 5:14).

That ye may be blameless and harmless, the sons of God, without rebuke, in the midst of a crooked and perverse nation, among whom ye shine as lights in the world;

Holding forth [give attention to] *the word of life...* (Philippians 2:15-16).

Ye are all the children [sons] *of light, and the children of the day...*(1 Thessalonians 5:5). Compare Ephesians 5:8-9.

We are the lights that He is Father of.

...with whom is no variableness, neither shadow of turning (James 1:17).

The Father (the Giver of the gift which we are) and the lights that He is Father of (the gift which we are) are marked by this final characteristic: there is "no variableness" nor "shadow of turning."

"Variableness" is the Greek word *parallage*[11], and it means, "transmutation (of phase or orbit), (figuratively) fickleness; variableness; change, variation." It is taken from *para* (beside) and *allasso* (to make different, to exchange one thing for another). It is used only here. *Vine's*[12] adds, compare the English, "parallax" (the difference between the directions of a body as seen from two different points); or "a transmission" (from one condition to another).

"*...no variation [rising from setting]...* (AMP).

"*...without change...*" (TLB).

"*...who does not change*" (NIV).

The Lord is steady and constant, and can be trusted, relied upon. He is faithful. His Spirit—that portion of Himself that underlies the gift which we are and the gifts which we have—empowers us to be like Him and to do the same!

But Thou art the same, and Thy years shall have no end (Psalm 102:27).

This literally reads, "Thou art He." It is the pronoun in the third person singular.

For I am the Lord, I change [alter] *not...*(Malachi 3:6).

Jesus Christ the same yesterday, and to day, and for ever (Hebrews 13:8).

This Greek rendering is, "Jesus Christ, He, Himself, the One." It is a reflexive pronoun in the third person singular.

In James 1:17, "shadow of turning" is taken from two Greek words.

First, "shadow" is *aposkiasma*[13], and it means, "a shading off; a shade casting one object on another." It is taken from *apo* (off, away from) and *skia* (shade or shadow caused by the interception of light, an image cast by an object and representing the form of that object; a sketch or outline).

Second, "turning" is *trope*[14], and it means, "to turn; a turn, revolution (figuratively, variation)." It is used with reference to the heavenly bodies, the revolution of the heavenly orbs. Consider these other translations:

"...who does not change like shifting shadows." (NIV)

"...who casts no shadow upon the earth." (Moffatt)

"...nor shadow of eclipse." (Montgomery)

No changes in this lower world can cast a shadow on the unchanging Fount of light. God is alike incapable of change, and incapable of being changed by the action of others!

With God *and* His people, you can count on receiving the real deal, the substance and not the shadow, unchanged by the circumstances of life. We are heavenly or spiritual beings, partakers of the ascended life. We stay in the orbit of His will![15]

The marks of this overcoming life are constancy, faithfulness, and stability. The fire on the Levitical altar was never to go out (Lev. 6:12-13). That fire originally came from heaven, from above. We are learning to flow in His abiding anointing every moment of every day.

We are learning the secrets of the ascended life. With a new perspective, we have looked at our fears and His favor through the eyes of God. We have begun to download and impart His life and love to others from the heavens.

Every one of you is a person of great influence. In your world, your metron, and your sphere of influence, you have been called to give away all that you are and all that you have.

The Lord Jesus, the Pattern Son, went so low to reach all of us that He can bring forth any human situation horizontally. It's time for you to "condescend," to yield or submit yourself to lowly things (Rom. 12:16).

In Jesus' name, I release the gift that you are and the gifts that you have!

There remains yet but one primary illustration of this divine impartation—the *application* of the ascended life. There is a wisdom from above...

ENDNOTES

1. James Strong. *Strong's Dictionary of Bible Words* (New York, New York: Nelson Reference, 1996), #5486.

2. Ibid., #1394.

3. W.E. Vine, Merrill F. Unger. *Vine's Complete Expository Dictionary of Old & New Testament Words* (Nashville: Nelson Reference, 1996).

4. The Greek word for "gift" in James 1:17 is *dosis* and is used in these other New Testament verses (see Matt. 5:42; 10:8; Luke 6:38; John 14:27; 1 John 3:1; and Rev. 3:21).

5. Strong, #13.

6. Ibid, #5046.

7. The Greek word for "perfect" in James 1:17 is *telios* and is used in these other New Testament verses: Romans 12:2; Colossians 1:28; 4:12; and James 1:4; 3:2.

8. Strong, #509.

9. Ibid, #2597.

10. Ibid, #5457.

11. Ibid, #3883.

12. Vine.

13. Strong, #644.

14. Ibid, #5157.

15. The purpose of a demon is to seduce us away from the government of God. The primary Greek word for "deceive" is *planao* (Strong #4105; compare the English word "planet"), and it means "to roam (from safety, truth, or

virtue); to cause to stray, to lead astray, to lead aside from the right way; to wander from the path, to roam about; be seduced." Those who partake of the ascended life remain faithful to the Covenant.

Chapter Seven

THE ASCENDED LIFE: ITS APPLICATION

I press toward the mark for the prize of the high calling of God in Christ Jesus (Philippians 3:14).

The high calling is the *ascended life.*

We have learned about the *secret* and the *perspective* of the ascended life. We have begun to download or impart His life and love to others from the Most Holy Place, giving away and sharing the gift that we are and the gifts that we have! Now we must *apply* the wisdom of these secrets to our everyday living.

THIS WISDOM IS FROM ABOVE

Wisdom has built her house; she has hewn out [to dig, to cut, to carve] *its seven pillars* (Proverbs 9:1, NIV). Compare 1 Timothy 3:5; Revelation 3:12.

Young man, how are you going to build your life? Your career? Your marriage? Your portfolio? Your business? Your ministry? Do you have a five-year plan?

Young mother, how are you going to build character into your children?

Pastor, how are you going to build your local church? Apostles and prophets, how are you going to build your teams?

The Bible explains itself; in its light we see light (Ps. 36:9). These "seven pillars" of Proverbs 9:1 are revealed by James' seven-fold description of the wisdom from above!

> *But the wisdom that is from above is first pure, then peaceable, gentle, and easy to be intreated, full of mercy and good fruits, without partiality, and without hypocrisy.*
>
> *And the fruit of righteousness is sown in peace of them that make peace* (James 3:17-18).
>
> *But the wisdom that comes from heaven is first of all pure; then peace-loving, considerate, submissive, full of mercy and good fruit, impartial and sincere.*
>
> *Peacemakers who sow in peace raise a harvest of righteousness* (James 3:17-18, NIV).
>
> *But the wisdom from above is first of all pure (undefiled); then it is peace-loving, courteous (considerate, gentle). [It is willing to] yield to reason, full of compassion and good fruits; it is wholehearted and straight-forward, impartial and unfeigned—free from doubts, wavering, and insincerity.*

And the harvest of righteousness (of conformity to God's
will in thought and deed) is [the fruit of the seed] sown in
peace by those who work for and make peace[in them-
selves and in others, that peace which means concord,
agreement, and harmony between individuals, with
undisturbedness, in a peaceful mind free from fears and
agitating passions and moral conflicts] (James 3:17-18,
AMP).

We have examined the secret, the perspective, and the
impartation of the ascended life. But the primary illustration
and catalyst (the dynamic, that which makes it work) to this
impartation is the *application* of the wisdom that is from
above!

This *application* of godly wisdom flows down from the
heavenly places, and makes for the daily answers to life's situations, to any and every circumstance—it gets the job done!
This is loosing Christ out into the streets. The Word must be
made flesh, walked out in shoe leather. The Gospel we
preach must work in the dirt.

These seven aspects of Christ-like wisdom (James 1:17)
are all traits of the new man created in His image and likeness,
and fully describe the characteristics of effective ministry.

The Lord GOD hath given me the tongue of the learned,
that I should know how to speak a word in season to him
that is weary: He wakeneth morning by morning, He
wakeneth mine ear to hear as the learned (Isaiah 50:4).

Wisdom is the right application of knowledge. Messiah and those conformed to His image have been given
"the tongue of the learned [disciple]." The New International
Version renders this to be the "instructed tongue."

Heaven's wisdom shows us "how to speak," what to speak ("a word"), when to speak ("in season"), and to whom to speak ("to him that is weary").

This expresses the ministry of the "peacemakers" (Matt. 5:9), mature sons, the king-priest ministry, also known as the "more excellent ministry" (Heb. 8:6).[1] These carry the peace of God, and have the ability to make or create peace. These can walk into a room and change the entire atmosphere. Empowered from above, a peacemaker can step in between two warring spirits, swallow up the death and hell in both, and not ever become contaminated!

Jesus, the Pattern Son, is the "prince of peace," the Benefactor of peace (Isa. 9:6). Our Lord is also the "king of peace," the Administrator of peace. He is looking for those who will be kings and priests with Him, ministering His life and love.

THIS WISDOM IS THE WISDOM OF CHRIST

The ascended life is *His* life. The wisdom from above is *His* wisdom. Christ *is* the wisdom of God (see Proverbs 8)

*But unto them which are called, both Jews and Greeks, Christ the power of God, and the **wisdom** of God* (1 Corinthians 1:24, Emphasis added).

*But of Him are ye in Christ Jesus, who of God is made unto us **wisdom**…*(1 Corinthians 1:30, Emphasis added).

*But we speak the **wisdom** of God in a mystery, even the hidden* [veiled] ***wisdom**, which God ordained before the world unto our glory* (1 Corinthians 2:7, Emphasis added). Compare Isaiah 48:6; Revelation 2:17.

In whom [Christ] *are hid* [veiled, stored up] *all the treasures of **wisdom** and knowledge* (Colossians 2:3, Emphasis added).

The word for "treasures" in this latter verse is *thesaurus,* and it means, "a deposit of wealth; a store-house (for safe keeping)." The Lord is the sum of all wisdom. He keeps it safe within Himself until you discover who He is in you! It is the glory of God to conceal a thing and the honor of kings to search out a matter (Prov. 25:2 with Rev. 1:6; 5:10). All wisdom is in Christ, and Christ is in and among all of you (Col. 1:27)!

The *application* of heavenly wisdom that flows down from the ascended life manifests as the daily answers to the stuff we deal with every day. There is no situation of life that this wisdom cannot touch, for in Him is hidden, or stored, all wisdom! Everything that we will ever need is stockpiled in this wisdom from above. Christ is the wisdom of God, and Christ is "in" us (Col. 1:27)! All we have to do is ask God.

If any of you lacks wisdom, he should ask God, who gives generously to all without finding fault, and it will be given to him (James 1:5, NIV).

To "lack" this wisdom is not to have it. We are not using what we already have! John's epistle declares that we know everything (1 John 2:20). We're just not fully aware of all that we know. Saints, get the information from God, and then get the confirmation from your leaders.

And all Israel heard of the judgment which the king [Solomon] *had judged; and they feared the king: for they saw that the wisdom of God was in him, to do judgment* (1 Kings 3:28).

Furthermore, the outstanding Old Testament figure who applied the wisdom from above was King Solomon. Others could see the wisdom of God that flowed through Him. Contrariwise, classical Kingdom-sonship theology has become weak in the earth because heretofore it has just been a "message." We have come to the time of birthing His eternal purposes throughout the nations, and all we have produced is a "wind of doctrine" (Eph. 4:14). The prophet Isaiah confirms that *we have not wrought any deliverance in the earth* (Isa. 26:18).

> *His intent was that now, through the church, the manifold* [variegated] *wisdom of God should be made known to the rulers and authorities in the heavenly realms* (Ephesians 3:10, NIV). Compare 1 Peter 4:10.

Like Joseph's colored coat with many folds (Gen. 37:3), God's wisdom and grace is layered. The primary New Testament instrument that has been commissioned to display this manifold wisdom is the Church, His many-membered Body. This is more than a message. We are to make His wisdom known.

THE SPIRIT OF WISDOM

Do you need an answer? The "word of wisdom" (1 Cor. 12:8), a fragment of His all-wisdom, is *the* answer to a given situation. But did you know that Jesus the Messiah was anointed with the very "spirit of wisdom"?

> *And there shall come forth a rod out of the stem of Jesse, and a Branch shall grow out of his roots:*
>
> *And the spirit of the Lord shall rest upon him, the spirit of wisdom and understanding, the spirit of counsel and*

might, the spirit of knowledge and of the fear of the Lord;
(Isaiah 11:1-2).

The Messianic "rod" in this passage is Jesus, who came out of David, the "stem" of Jesse. The "branch" that grows out of His roots is His offspring, the Church (John 15:1-5). The Spirit of the Lord, along with the spirit of wisdom, shall rest upon "him" (Christ the Head *and* Body), "him that overcometh" (Rev. 2:7,17; 3:12,21).

Jesus and His glorious Church are anointed with the fullness of the Spirit (John 3:34), "the seven spirits" of God enumerated in Isaiah 11:1-2.[2] This seven-fold anointing, including "the spirit of wisdom," rested upon Jesus. His mantle is falling upon us, and through us His wisdom is being sent apostolically into all the earth (2 Kings 2:13-14 with Rev. 5:6).

Like the healing balm (salve) of Gilead (Jer. 8:22), we are God's applied medicine that ministers to a hurting and broken humanity (Prov. 17:22; Ezek. 47:12). We embody the fiery wisdom that comes down from Heaven as the "answer" of God (1 Kings 18:24). My friend, you have been filled with His wisdom. You are carrying answers for all those who live in your world. Arm and equip yourself with a fresh awareness of who you are, where you're from, and what you've got!

Wisdom's Seven Pillars

Again, James' seven-fold description of this heavenly wisdom constitutes the "seven pillars" of Proverbs 9:1. This *application*, the kind and quality of these wise answers to life's questions, will bear the following marks.

*But the wisdom that is from above is first **pure**...*(James 3:17, Emphasis added).

To begin with, this wisdom is "first" (in time, place, order, or importance) pure." This is the word *hagnos*[3], and it means, "clean, innocent, modest, perfect; exciting reverence, venerable, sacred; pure from carnality, chaste, modest; pure from fault and mixture, immaculate." It is also rendered in the King James Version as, "chaste, clear."

For I am jealous over you with godly jealousy: for I have espoused you to one husband, that I may present you as a chaste virgin to Christ (2 Corinthians 11:2).

Finally, brethren, whatsoever things are true, whatsoever things are honest, whatsoever things are just, whatsoever things are pure, whatsoever things are lovely, whatsoever things are of good report; if there be any virtue, and if there be any praise, think on these things (Philippians 4:8).

Beloved, now are we the sons of God, and it doth not yet appear what we shall be: but we know that, when He shall appear, we shall be like Him; for we shall see Him as He is. And every man that hath this hope in Him purifieth himself, even as He is pure (1 John 3:2-3).

The wise answers we minister from the heavens are always pure. This forever delivers those who shrink back in fear, wondering, "But what if I might say something wrong? I wouldn't want people to misunderstand me." He and His wisdom are pure from fault and mixture.

Young people, every answer that a godly father or mother gives to their children is clean and right. Brothers and sisters, every answer that a godly shepherd gives to the sheep is pure.

*But the wisdom that is from above is...then **peaceable**...* (James 3:17, Emphasis added).

Second, the wisdom from above is "peaceable." This is the word *eirenikos*[4], and it means, "pacific; by implication, salutary; loving peace." It is only used in one other place, and has to do with the disciplines of God.

> *Now no chastening for the present seemeth to be joyous, but grievous: nevertheless afterward it yieldeth the peaceable fruit of righteousness unto them which are exercised thereby* (Hebrews 12:11).

> *No discipline seems pleasant at the time, but painful. Later on, however, it produces a harvest of righteousness and peace for those who have been trained by it* (Hebrews 12:11, NIV).

Did your parents discipline you? Do you discipline your own children? This is always to be done with the wisdom of God. I've met a lot of adults, even preachers, who have never been "trained."

> *But the wisdom that is from above is...**gentle**...*(James 3:17, Emphasis added).

Third, heavenly wisdom is "gentle." This is the word *epieikes*[5], and it means, "appropriate, (by implication) mild; seemingly, suitable, equitable, fitting, fair, mild, moderate, forbearing; sweet reasonableness, not insisting on the letter of the law." It expresses that considerateness that looks humanely and reasonably at the facts of a case—it is fair. It is also rendered in the King James Version as, "moderation, patient."

> *Let your moderation be known unto all men. The Lord is at hand* (Philippians 4:5).

Not given to wine, no striker, not greedy of filthy lucre; but patient, not a brawler, not covetous (1 Timothy 3:3). Compare Titus 3:2.

Servants, be subject to your masters with all fear; not only to the good and gentle, but also to the froward (1 Peter 2:18).

Many of life's situations could be solved with the application of "sweet reasonableness." *A soft* (tender, delicate) *answer turns away wrath, but grievous* (harsh) *words stir up anger* (Prov. 15:1). The New International Version renders this, "a gentle answer."

This wise gentleness does not insist on the letter of the law, nor does it demand to always have its own way. Are you a considerate person, regarding the needs, weaknesses, and strengths of others?

Timothy knew that this kind of patience had to be in the life of every elder and minister. Christian leaders are called to solve the problem, not create even more trouble. Godly "masters" or employers know how to apply this kind of wisdom with all their employees.

*But the wisdom that is from above is...**easy to be intreated**...*(James 3:17, Emphasis added).

Fourth, this wisdom from above is "easy to be intreated." This is the word *eupeithes*[6] (used only here), and it means, "good for persuasion, (intransitively) compliant, easily obeying; ready to obey." It is derived from *eu* (good, well) and *peitho* (to convince; to assent to evidence or authority; to rely by inward certainty, to believe; to be persuaded, to have confidence).

Can you be corrected? Are you submissive in your spirit, ready to obey? When Heaven's answer is applied to your particular situation, are you willing to yield? God's Spirit and Word are always in agreement. When confronted with truth, will you let your mind be renewed, or will you dig in your heels and hold on to your previous teachings?

> But the wisdom that is from above is...*full of mercy and good fruits*...(James 3:17, Emphasis added).

Fifth, godly wisdom is "full (replete) of mercy and good fruits." "Mercy" is the Greek word *eleos*[7], and it means, "compassion; kindness or good will toward the miserable and the afflicted, joined with a desire to help them." *Vine's* adds, "the outward manifestation of pity; it assumes need on the part of him who receives it, and resources adequate to meet the need on the part of him who shows it."[8]

Eleos is used 28 times in the New Testament, including the following verses, emphasis added:

> Through the tender **mercy** of our God; whereby the dayspring (dawn, the rising of the sun) from on high hath visited us (Luke 1:78).

> But God, who is rich in **mercy**...(Ephesians 2:4).

> Not by works of righteousness which we have done, but according to His **mercy** He saved us, by the washing of regeneration, and renewing of the Holy Ghost; (Titus 3:5).

> Let us therefore come boldly unto the throne of grace, that we may obtain **mercy**, and find grace to help in time of need (Hebrews 4:16).

*Blessed be the God and Father of our Lord Jesus Christ, which according to His abundant **mercy** hath begotten us again unto a lively hope by the resurrection of Jesus Christ from the dead* (1 Peter 1:3).

Do you want to help people? You carry a wisdom that is from above. Every day we meet folks who are crying out. They don't know what to do. They don't know God. Many of God's own people know His acts, but remain ignorant of His ways (Ps. 103:7). People are scared, and are struggling. But you are full of mercy. You are their answer.

The word translated as "good" in James 3:17 is *agathos*, the same word used in James 1:17, the key verse from Chapter Six.

The word for "fruits" is *karpos*[9], and it means, "fruit (as plucked); what originates or comes from something, an effect, a result; work, act, deed." *Vine's* adds that "fruit" is "that which is produced by the inherent energy of a living organism; the visible expression of power working inwardly and invisibly, the character of the 'fruit' being evidence of the character of the power producing it."[10]

Karpos is used 66 times in the Greek text, including the following verses, emphasis added:

*Ye shall know them by their **fruits**. Do men gather grapes of thorns, or figs of thistles? Even so every good tree bringeth forth good **fruit**...*(Matthew 7:16-17).

*Ye have not chosen Me, but I have chosen you, and ordained you, that ye should go and bring forth **fruit**, and that your **fruit** should remain: that whatsoever ye shall ask of the Father in My name, He may give it you* (John 15:16).

*But the **fruit** of the Spirit is love, joy, peace, longsuffering, gentleness, goodness, faith, meekness, temperance: against such there is no law* (Galatians 5:22-23).

*(For the **fruit** of the Spirit is in all goodness and righteousness and truth)* (Ephesians 5:9).

*Be patient therefore, brethren, unto the **coming** of the Lord. Behold, the husbandman waiteth for the precious **fruit** of the earth, and hath long patience for it, until He receive the early and latter rain* (James 5:7).

You are full of good fruit, full of His life and wisdom. You were picked out to be picked on. Busy people are fruitful people. Their tree is loaded. They have much to give, and are willing to give it.

*But the wisdom that is from above is...**without partiality**...*(James 3:17, Emphasis added).

Sixth, divine wisdom is "without partiality." This is the word *adiakritos*[11] (used only here), and it means, "undistinguished, (actively) impartial; unintelligible, without dubiousness, ambiguity, or uncertainty; without variance." It is derived from *a* (the negative particle) and *diakrino* (to separate thoroughly, to discriminate, decide, discern, judge).

Christ is not prejudiced (Gal. 3:28). The wisdom from above knows no prejudice. God's wise answers refuse to take sides—He is for Himself! He is no respecter of persons, literally, "of faces" (Acts 10:34-35).[12]

All prejudice is from beneath, and is to be swallowed by the wisdom that is from above. Men and women raise these issues and build these walls—male and female, black and white, clergy and laity, old and young (the generation gap), educated and uneducated, rich and poor, or masters (employers) and servants (employees).

Jesus is wonderful. He loves us all. His wisdom consumes every warring spirit.

The Gospel of the Kingdom touches every class of people. When Paul and Silas ministered at Philippi (Acts 16), they reached out to every level: the upper class, as seen in Lydia the businesswoman; the middle class, represented by the jailor and his family; and the lower class, as exampled by the demonized slave girl whom the Lord delivered.

Real orthodoxy is impartial. It can be preached in every nation and to all peoples. Otherwise, fads (what's hot and what's not) come and go, and are not part of reformational truth. Godly wisdom is consistent. We must apply it to every situation.

*But the wisdom that is from above is...**without** **hypocrisy*** (James 3:17, Emphasis added).

Finally, the wisdom from above is "without hypocrisy." This is the Greek word *anupokritos*[13], and it means, "undissembled, sincere; unfeigned, undisguised." It is also rendered in the King James Version as "without dissimulation (hypocrisy), unfeigned."

Let love be without dissimulation...(Romans 12:9).

By pureness, by knowledge, by longsuffering, by kindness, by the Holy Ghost, by love unfeigned (2 Corinthians 6:6). Compare 1 Peter 1:22.

Now the end of the commandment is charity out of a pure heart, and of a good conscience, and of faith unfeigned (1 Timothy 1:5). Compare 2 Timothy 1:5.

Every answer from God, marked by godly wisdom, is honest and sincere. It wears no mask, no disguise.

But if ye have bitter envying and strife in your hearts, glory not, and lie not against the truth.

This wisdom descendeth not from above, but is earthly, sensual, devilish.

For where envying and strife is, there is confusion and every evil work (James 3:14-16).

The wisdom from above (the Christ nature) is first pure. Everything outside of Christ is a lying vanity. The wisdom from beneath is earthly, sensual, and even demonic.

"The way of life is above to the wise that he may depart from hell beneath" (Prov. 15:24)—the dust realm, that which is earthy. This way of life from above is the way of the eagle (Prov. 30:19).

And hath raised us up together, and made us sit together in heavenly places in Christ Jesus: (Ephesians 2:6).

The *secret* of the ascended life is our union with Him, our fellowship with Christ and our protection in Christ. If you never see your worth in Christ, you will rob the earth of your reason for breathing. We have the mind of Christ. We live in the heavenlies.

[The Bridegroom is speaking] *Come look with me...from the top of Amana...*(Song of Solomon 4:8).

The *perspective* of the ascended life has brought a new view of our fears, our enemies and His favor, His blessings. That new viewpoint brings a whole new mindset and vocabulary. We see everyone and everything through the eyes of God. The Christian has a whole new worldview.

Do everything without complaining or arguing,

so that you may become blameless and pure, children of God without fault in a crooked and depraved generation, in which you shine like stars in the universe

as you hold out the word of life...(Philippians 2:14-16, NIV).

The *impartation* of the ascended life reaches out to everyone in our world. We download the gift that we are and the gifts that we have.

Now that we understand where we are and how our renewed minds think, we are ready to minister every good thing that is in us (Philem. 1:6). Once we hear this word of present truth (2 Pet. 1:12), we will never be the same. Without fear, we touch others.

Wisdom is the principal [first, best, chief] *thing; therefore get wisdom...*(Proverbs 4:7).

The fear of the Lord is the beginning of wisdom... (Proverbs 9:10).

The *application* of the ascended life is the wisdom of Heaven for the situations of earth. Every answer is in Him, and He has hidden Himself in you (Col. 1:27; 2:3). Christ in you is the best-kept secret in your entire world. In the day when all things are headed up in Christ (Eph. 1:10), He has purposed to manifest, display, exhibit, and apply His wisdom in and through a many-membered, corporate Church.

He now comes to show up, show out, and show off through His Church, the hiding place of His manifold, multifaceted wisdom.

I hear this calling. Do you?

I hear the Lord ask, "Is there anyone who will come up here, live with Me, breathe with Me?

"Is there anyone who will ascend and listen to Me talk, and then repeat what I say with the same spirit?

"Is there anyone who will come up here? I have wisdom. I *am* wisdom. The answer for cancer...the answer for AIDS...the answer to poverty in all of its forms...the answer to racism...every answer can only be found in one place— they are all hidden in Me....

"Is there anyone who will come up here?"

Jesus is the ascended One. We now view all things from His perspective. Jesus' life is the life we impart. Jesus is the wisdom from above.

THE NATIONS ARE COMING

The Church of Jesus Christ is to be salt and light, a witness to the nations of the earth (Matt. 5:13-16; Acts 1:8).

And when the queen of Sheba heard of the fame of Solomon concerning the name of the Lord, she came to prove [test] him with hard questions.

And she came to Jerusalem with a very great train, with camels that bare spices, and very much gold, and precious stones: and when she was come to Solomon, she communed with him of all that was in her heart.

And Solomon told her all her questions: there was not any thing hid from the king, which he told her not.

And when the queen of Sheba had seen all Solomon's wisdom, and the house that he had built,

And the meat of his table, and the sitting of his servants, and the attendance of his ministers, and their apparel, and his cupbearers, and his ascent by which he went up unto the house of the Lord; there was no more spirit in her.

And she said to the king, It was a true report that I heard in mine own land of thy acts and of thy wisdom.

Howbeit I believed not the words, until I came, and mine eyes had seen it: and, behold, the half was not told me...

And she gave the king an hundred and twenty talents of gold, and of spices very great store, and precious stones: there came no more such abundance of spices as these which the queen of Sheba gave to king Solomon (1 Kings 10:1-7,10).

Then you [God's people] will look and be radiant, your heart will throb and swell with joy; the wealth on the seas will be brought to you, to you the riches of the nations will come (Isaiah 60:5, NIV)

The Queen of the South will rise at the judgment with this generation and condemn it; for she came from the ends of the earth to listen to Solomon's wisdom, and now one greater than Solomon is here (Matthew 12:42, NIV).

The *application* of the ascended life is "the wisdom from above" (James 3:17). The Queen of Sheba, hearing of the wisdom of King Solomon, came from Egypt to test him with "hard questions." This word in First Kings 10:1 means, "a riddle, a difficult question, a perplexing saying or question, a parable."

The queen was thoroughly impressed with Solomon's wisdom (he made known her questions and answers) and the order of his house and Kingdom. But she was completely overwhelmed when she beheld "...*his ascent by which he went up unto the house of the Lord; there was no more spirit in her*" (1 Kings 10:5). The word for "ascent" in this latter verse is *o-law'*, the word for the Burnt Offering or Ascending Offering explained in Chapter Two!

I can almost hear Solomon say, "O queen, you have only seen the natural half; the other half is yet to be told (announced) in the unseen realm of the Spirit. I am but a mere human king, a picture of the Messiah who is to come. It will be the revelation of *His* ascension and coronation that will move and impact all nations with the overwhelming presence of God."

> *And it shall come to pass in the last days, that the mountain of the Lord's house shall be established in the top of the mountains, and shall be exalted above the hills; and all nations shall flow* [stream] *unto it* (Isaiah 2:2).

Jesus, the One who is "greater than Solomon," is here! The nations are coming to Him as they are being drawn to the House of the Lord, the end-time Church. As they flow up to Zion, the Church (Heb. 12:22-23), they will behold the ascended life and wisdom of the Corporate Church and consequently offer their riches, creating a massive transfer of wealth (Prov. 13:22).

> *And the city* [Church] *had no need of the sun, neither of the moon, to shine in it: for the glory of God did lighten it, and the Lamb is the light thereof.*

SECRETS OF THE ASCENDED LIFE

And the nations of them which are saved shall walk in the light of it: and the kings of the earth do bring their glory and honour [valuables] *into it* (Revelation 21:23-24).

This world is in a crucible. Nations are at their boiling point. The need for real answers has never been greater. There is only one way to overcome it—we must get above it! We must show them how to ascend into Zion.

Now is the time to arise, to ascend. Now is the time to be strengthened and empowered by His life. Now is the time to *look through the eyes of God....*

ENDNOTES

1. For an in-depth study of the "more excellent ministry" (Heb. 8:6), read my book by the same title.

2. The "seven spirits of God" (Rev. 1:4; 3:1; 4:5; 5:6) is a biblical expression denoting the fullness of the Spirit, the Spirit "without measure" (John 3:34). The Holy Ghost Baptism, the Pentecostal experience, is not the fullness of the Spirit. It is rather the "firstfrusts" of the Spirit (Rom. 8:23) and the "earnest" of our inheritance (Eph. 1:13-14). For an in-depth teaching about the "seven spirits of God" and the Man whose name is the Branch, see my book *The Tabernacle of Jesus, Volume Two* (in connection with the Golden Candlestick or Lampstand). Call our church office at 910-324-5026 or visit our Website (www.kelleyvarner.org).

3. James Strong. *Strong's Dictionary of Bible Words* (New York, New York: Nelson Reference, 1996), #53.

4. Ibid., #1516.

5. Ibid., #1933.

6. Ibid., #2138.

7. Ibid., #1656.

8. W.E. Vine, Merrill F. Unger. *Vine's Complete Expository Dictionary of Old & New Testament Words* (Nashville: Nelson Reference, 1996).

9. Strong, #2590.

10. Vine.

11. Strong, #87

12. Both Testaments testify that God is no respecter of persons (see Deut. 10:17; 16:19: 2 Chron. 19:7; Job 34:19; Ps. 82:1-2; Matt. 22:16; Luke 20:21; Rom. 2:11; Gal. 2:6; Eph. 6:9; Col. 3:11,25; James 2:4; and 1 Pet. 1:17).

13. Strong, #505.

LOOKING THROUGH THE EYES OF GOD

...I press on to take hold of that for which Christ Jesus took hold of me.

Brothers, I do not consider myself yet to have taken hold of it. But one thing I do: Forgetting what is behind and straining toward what is ahead,

I press on toward the goal to win the prize for which God has called me heavenward in Christ Jesus (Philippians 3:12-14, NIV).

There *is* a high calling....

There is an overcoming remnant, a governmental people who have pressed their way to the top of Mount Zion. These men and women are partakers of the "divine nature" (2 Pet. 1:4), of His character and "more excellent ministry" (Heb. 8:6).

An Overview of the Ascended Life

This volume, the sequel to my previous writing, *Sound the Alarm*, has set forth in-depth the Kingdom principle that this high calling is also known as the *ascended life*.

When Christ, who is our life, shall appear, then shall ye also appear with Him in glory (Colossians 3:4).

Chapter One laid the foundation of this Christo-centric truth: the ascended life is *His* life. Jesus' work is finished (John 19:30). He has "ascended up far above all heavens, that He might fill all things" with Himself. We have ascended with Him (Eph. 2:6). Christ is from above. Adam is from beneath. He is raising us up in this Third Day!

Chapters Two and Three explained the two major Old Testament typological pictures of the ascended life. The Burnt Offering was also known as the *Ascending Offering*. The Lord's portion in this primary sacrifice was the entire offering—God got all of it! Moreover, Psalms 120-134, the pilgrim Songs of the Goings Up, the Songs of the Steps, are also named the *Psalms of Ascent*. Grace is a progression (2 Pet. 3:18). We are being saved (2 Cor. 1:10).

Hast thou heard the secret of God?...(Job 15:8).

Chapter Four showed us the *secret* of the ascended life. This revelation has to be birthed in your spirit by the Holy Spirit. Joined to the Lord in blood covenant, we are one spirit with Him who has ascended. We are in union with the ascended One.

For our conversation [citizenship] *is in heaven; from whence also we look...*(Philippians 3:20).

Chapter Five unfolded the *perspective* of the ascended life. Once we receive this revelatory insight that we have ascended with Him, we immediately begin to see everything and everyone differently. From God's point of view, we behold our fears (our enemies) and His favor (His blessings).

Every good gift and every perfect gift is from above, and cometh down from the Father of lights, with whom is no variableness, neither shadow of turning (James 1:17).

Chapter Six emphasized the *impartation* of the ascended life. We have ascended with Him. We are one with Him and have received a new perspective of everything and everyone. Only then can we begin to download and minister His life and love to others from the Heavens. We impart to others the gift that we are and the gifts that we have!

But the wisdom that is from above is first pure, then peaceable, gentle, and easy to be intreated, full of mercy and good fruits, without partiality, and without hypocrisy (James 3:17).

Chapter Seven further illustrated this impartation. The wisdom from above is the *application* of the ascended life, supplying daily answers to life's situations.

THE EYES OF THE LORD

Having summarized these secrets of the ascended life, we close this volume by examining the phrase: *Looking Through the Eyes of God*.

The Old Testament has much to say about the "eyes of the Lord." All the verses below underscore the blessings and benefits of viewing all things from His perspective[1], emphasis added:

137

*But Noah found grace in the **eyes** of the Lord* (Genesis 6:8).

Noah found another age in God's eyes. Looking through the eyes of God provides us insight into His unfolding plan of redemption.

*A land which the Lord thy God careth for: the **eyes** of the Lord thy God are always upon it...*(Deuteronomy 11:12).

We behold God's inheritance as we look through His eyes. In the New Testament, His inheritance is His people.

*And the king said unto Zadok, Carry back the ark of God into the city: if I shall find favour in the **eyes** of the Lord, He will bring me again, and show me both it, and His habitation:* (2 Samuel 15:25).

As with King David, we see the revelation of His favor unto Zion when we view His purposes through His eyes.

*For the **eyes** of the Lord run to and fro throughout the whole earth, to show Himself strong in the behalf of them whose heart is perfect toward Him...*(2 Chronicles 16:9).

Only by looking at others through the eyes of the Lord can we rightly discern those who are His. The eyes of the Lord see the heart.

*The **eyes** of the Lord are upon the righteous...*(Psalm 34:15).

The eyes of the Lord discern the difference between righteousness and unrighteousness, between the precious and the vile (Jer. 15:19). Compare Proverbs 15:3.

Looking Through the Eyes of God

*The **eyes** of the Lord preserve knowledge...*(Proverbs 22:12).

The New International Version says, "The eyes of the Lord keep watch over knowledge..." All true knowledge and understanding can only be discovered through the eyes of the Lord.

*For who hath despised the day of small things? for they shall rejoice, and shall see the plummet in the hand of Zerubbabel with those seven; they are the **eyes** of the Lord, which run to and fro through the whole earth* (Zechariah 4:10).

Those who see everyone and everything through the eyes of the Lord have a global vision for all nations.

Those who partake of the ascended life are called to the top of the mountain to share His perspective, to look through the eyes of God.

The primary Hebrew word for *look* means, "to see, to look at, to inspect, to perceive, or to consider." The Old Testament is full of examples of how He looks at things, emphasis added:

*And God **looked** upon the earth, and, behold, it was corrupt; for all flesh had corrupted His way upon the earth* (Genesis 6:12).

*And God **looked** upon the children of Israel, and God had respect [to acknowledge] unto them* (Exodus 2:25).

*For He hath **looked** down from the height of His sanctuary; from heaven did the Lord behold the earth;* (Psalm 102:19).

For all those things hath mine hand made, and those things have been, saith the Lord: but to this man will I look, even to him that is poor and of a contrite spirit, and trembleth at my word (Isaiah 66:2).

THE EYES OF JESUS ARE THE LOOK OF GOD[2]

In the New Testament, the eyes of God are the eyes of Jesus. He is the express image and character of the Father (Heb. 1:3). Jesus' eyes are as a flame of fire.

And I saw heaven opened, and behold a white horse; and He that sat upon him was called Faithful and True, and in righteousness He doth judge and make war.

His eyes were as a flame of fire, and on His head were many crowns; and He had a name written, that no man knew, but He Himself.

And He was clothed with a vesture dipped in blood: and His name is called The Word of God (Revelation 19:11-13). Compare Daniel 10:6 with Revelation 1:14; 2:18 and John 1:1.

The eyes of God are the eyes of Jesus. The eyes of Jesus are the look of God. John declared, "...as He is, so are we in this world" (1 John 4:17; compare John 20:21). The Church is now the corporate expression of His hands and feet. The eyes of Jesus have become the eyes of His overcoming people. We are privileged to look at everyone and everything through the eyes of God. We need to look as He looked, emphasis added:

*And when He had taken the five loaves and the two fishes, He **looked** up to heaven, and blessed, and brake the loaves, and gave them to His disciples to set before them; and the two fishes divided he among them all* (Mark 6:41).

*And when Jesus came to the place, He **looked** up, and saw him, and said unto him, Zacchaeus, make haste, and come down; for to day I must abide at thy house* (Luke 19:5).

*And the Lord turned, and **looked** upon Peter. And Peter remembered the word of the Lord, how He had said unto him, Before the cock crow, thou shalt deny Me thrice* (Luke 22:61).

Those who live the ascended life look through the eyes of God, the eyes of Jesus. Our citizenship is in the heavens, from whence we look. His worldview is now our worldview. His value system is now our value system. As partakers of the divine nature, we love what He loves, and we hate what He hates.

WHERE WILL YOU BE IN THAT DAY?

To him that overcometh will I grant to sit with Me in My throne, even as I also overcame, and am set down with My Father in His throne (Revelation 3:21).

After this I beheld, and, lo, a great multitude, which no man could number, of all nations, and kindreds, and people, and tongues, stood before the throne, and before the Lamb, clothed with white robes, and palms in their hands...

Therefore are they before the throne of God, and serve Him day and night in His temple: and He that sitteth on the throne shall dwell among them...

For the Lamb which is in the midst of the throne shall feed them, and shall lead them unto living fountains of

waters: and God shall wipe away all tears from their eyes
(Revelation 7:9,15,17).

In the Book of Revelation, there are two classes of people. The corporate Overcomer, the company who pursues the high calling and the ascended life, sits with the Lord *in* His throne. There is also a vast multitude that stands *before* His throne.

But speaking the truth in love, may grow up into Him in all things, which is the head, even Christ: (Ephesians 4:15).

This is profound, but there is a people who will have matured into the place of His headship—there is a Headship Company! Those who press toward the mark of the high calling and the ascended life are partakers of His "divine nature" (2 Pet. 1:4). In Chapter Five these were invited to share His perspective from the "top" (head) of the mountain (Song of Solomon 4:8).

If we endure, we will also reign [be co-regent] *with Him. If we disown Him, He will also disown us;* (2 Timothy 2:12, NIV).

And hast made us unto our God kings and priests: and we shall reign on the earth (Revelation 5:10).

Not everybody is going to rule and reign with Him.[3] Again, in the Apocalypse, there is a crowd *in* the throne and there is a crowd *before* the throne.

The crowd that was *before* Him was weeping because they finally beheld what they could have had with those who were *in* the throne. Though invited to the high calling, they had not been willing to pay the price. They had not been wise to seek the way of life above. Instead, they had settled for the lesser realms. Some seem determined to live, to talk, and to think in the death and hell beneath (Prov. 15:24) rather than the heavens above.

If you are called to be best, and you are content to be good, that makes you fair.

Are you miserable? Are you struggling? Are you unfulfilled? If so, you have been called to live in a higher realm than your present condition.

You are not running from God, but are you hiding from God?

Have you been apprehended for the high calling, the ascended life?

Where will *you* be in that day?

You don't have to live in the hell beneath. Don't blame God. Don't blame the devil. And don't get upset with the preacher.

If you have been predestined to be *in* the throne, and you end up *before* the throne, you will weep...

For almost 40 years, I have ministered this Gospel of the Kingdom and the high calling to thousands of preachers. Some pastor churches of 20 members, and some pastor churches of over 20,000. In many of their eyes, I have seen a far-away look. Many have backed off from "present truth" (2 Pet. 1:12). Some have fainted.

Why? With the word of the Kingdom, there is no plan "B." There is plan "A" and there is plan "A."

Jonah, you are going to Nineveh! You can go God's way— He will pay the fare, or you can go your way—you will pay the fare (Jonah 1:3)! It will cost you. That angry, reluctant prophet turned his back on God and ran all the way to Tarshish, which some have rendered as, "the place of the breaking."

God's man went "down" to Joppa, "down" into the ship headed for Tarshish, "down" into the lowest parts of the ship, and (after the mariners had thrown him overboard) "down" to the depths of the sea (Jonah 1:3,5; 2:6). When a man runs from God, he creates a storm for everybody else. We cannot have covenant with God on our own terms.

Jonah went down to the place he called "hell," hell beneath. Jonah, you are going to Nineveh—there is a connecting flight! The great fish swallowed him up, and in that "belly of hell" (Jonah 2:2), the prophet began to pray. Jonah's praise made hell throw up!

Today is the day of salvation. Make a choice. Change your mind. Make your calling and election sure. How long does it take for you to say, "Yes"?

Which way will you have it? Where will *you* be in that day?

Arise, shine; for thy light is come, and the glory of the Lord is risen upon thee (Isaiah 60:1).

Since, then, you have been raised with Christ, set your hearts on things above, where Christ is seated at the right hand of God.

Set your minds on things above, not on earthly things (Colossians 3:1-2, NIV).

So if you're serious about living this new resurrection life with Christ, act like it. Pursue the things over which

Christ presides. Don't shuffle along, eyes to the ground, absorbed with the things right in front of you.

Look up, and be alert to what is going on around Christ—that's where the action is. See things from His perspective (Colossians 3:1-2, The Message Bible).

Once and for all, settle it in your heart.

There *is* a high calling.

Start today.

Arise and ascend!

Seek those things which are above, the *secrets of the ascended life....*

ENDNOTES

1. Besides those listed in the text, there are other Old Testament passages that talk about "the eyes of the Lord" (see Deut. 13:18; 1 Sam. 26:24; 1 Kings 5:5; 15:11; 16:25; 22:43; 2 Chron. 14:2; 21:6; 29:6; Prov. 5:21; Isa. 49:5; and Jer. 52:2).

2. The eyes of Jesus constitute the look of God. Note these places in the Gospels where Jesus "looked" (see Mark 3:5,34; 5:32; 6:41; 8:24,33; 10:23; Luke 1:25; 9:38; 19:5; 21:1). It is also noteworthy to consider what "Jesus saw" (see Matt. 4:21; 8:14,18; 9:9,22,36; 21:19; Mark 1:10,16,19; 2:5,14; 6:48; 9:14,25; 10:14; 12:34; Luke 5:20; 13:12; 17:14; 18:24; 21:2; and John 1:47; 5:6; 9:1).

3. The Greek word for "reign" is *basileuo* (Strong #936), and it means "to rule; to be king, to exercise kingly power, to reign; metaphorically, to exercise the highest influence, to control" (see Luke 1:33; Rom. 5:17,21; 1 Cor. 15:25; 1 Tim. 6:15; and Rev. 11:15,17; 19:6; 20:4,6; 22:5).

Resources

My original four messages on The Ascended Life are available on four cassettes for an offering of $18 (plus $6 shipping), or on four CDs for an offering of $24 (plus $8 shipping) through our church office. Call 910-324-5026 or E-mail: praiztab1@earthlink.net for more information.

The Spirit Word Channel

Dr. Kelley Varner and Praise Tabernacle Ministries can be viewed on-line daily at 5:00 AM EST. and 6:30 PM EST. Go to www.spiritwordchannel.org or link from our Website www.kelleyvarner.org.

CAROLINA LEADERSHIP INST.
(CLI)
(A Third Day Finishing School)

CAROLINA LEADERSHIP INSTITUTE is a vision and concept of an apostolic burden and mandate to impart the "word of the Kingdom" to the Carolinas and the nations.

> Acts 19:8-10 NIV
>
> *Paul entered the synagogue and spoke boldly there for three months, arguing persuasively about the kingdom of God.*
>
> *But some of them became obstinate; they refused to believe and publicly maligned the way. So Paul left them. He took the disciples with him and had discussions daily in the lecture hall of Tyrannus.*
>
> *This went on for two years, so that all the Jews and Greeks who lived in the province of Asia heard the word of the Lord.*

Our short-term goal is to impart a biblical foundation for understanding and expressing Kingdom principles through periodic weekend seminars called "Kingdom Institutes." The participants for these initial "Institutes" will be drawn from five fold ministries and other church leaders throughout the Eastern Carolina region.

Our long-term goal is to establish a School of the Bible through which a residential and on-line course of study would equip individuals for Kingdom ministry. This more traditional approach to Bible training would reach out to individuals who are answering a vocational call to ministry and those who seek to be more equipped for ministry in their local church setting.

Contact information:
CAROLINA LEADERSHIP INSTITUTE
Wendall S. Ward, Jr.
P.O. Box 1599
Richlands, NC 28574
Phone: 910.324.5026
E-mail: CLI2002@earthlink.net

OTHER RESOURSES
BY
—— KELLEY VARNER ——

TAPE CATALOG

To receive a full listing of Pastor Varner's books and tapes (audio and video), or information about our Tape of the Month and Seminars and Conferences, write or call for our current catalog:

PRAISE TABERNACLE

P.O. Box 785
Richlands, NC 28574-0785

Phone: 910-324-5026 or 324-5027
FAX: 910-324-1048

E-mail: praiztab1@earthlink.net
OR kvarner2@earthlink.net

Internet: www.kelleyvarner.org (Order on-line), or
www.ptmrichlands.org

E-MAIL NEWSLETTER

Subscribe to Pastor Varner's weekly E-mail newsletter, "The Praise Report," a resource for leaders, at www.kelleyvarner.org

TAPE OF THE MONTH

Two cassette tapes (including sermon notes) by Pastor Varner and other ministries are available each month on a monthly or annual offering basis. Write or call to join this growing family of listeners.

CONFERENCES AND SEMINARS

A variety of regional and national gatherings happen throughout the year here at Praise Tabernacle and the Crystal Coast Conference Center. Pastor Varner and the apostolic ministry team at Praise Tabernacle are also available for ministry in your church and local area.

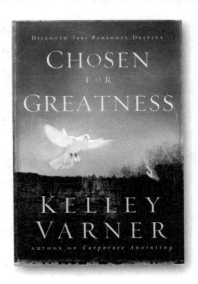

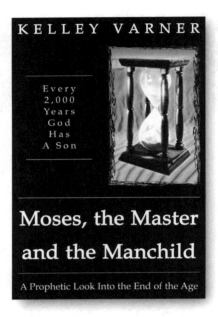

MOSES, THE MASTER, AND THE MANCHILD

The seed is buried in the bed of humanity. It grew out of Moses. It blossomed in the Son and it is to be revealed in the Manchild-the mature, victorious Church of the end of the age. You are about to be given prophetic keys that unlock the mysteries of the end times. Discover how Moses, our Lord Jesus, and the mighty victorious Church of the last days paint a picture of hope, power, and glory for God's people. You will be left breathless as this prophetic writer cuts through the confusion and fear surrounding the times in which we live. Be prepared to see and understand the end of the age like never before. Be prepared to discover your role during the most incredible time in history to be alive.

ISBN 0-7684-2121-7

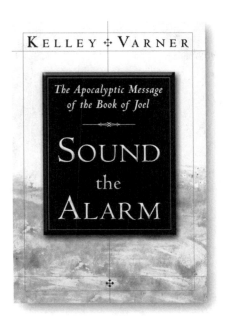

SOUND THE ALARM

Are you burning with a passion to pursue the "high call" of God and earn the eternal prize? *Sound the Alarm* is a prophetic cry to forsake religious tradition and usher in a "Third Day" revelation of the Lord. Discover how to sanctify yourself to His purpose to emerge from desolation, consecration and reformation as a champion for Christ. Now is the time for the Church to return to the power of preaching a pure Gospel. With its in-depth look at the Book of Joel, *Sound the Alarm* sounds the trumpet for a radical movement of apostolic reform.

ISBN 0-7684-2272-8

Additional copies of this book and other
book titles from DESTINY IMAGE are
available at your local bookstore.

For a complete list of our titles,
visit us at www.destinyimage.com
Send a request for a catalog to:

Destiny Image® Publishers, Inc.
P.O. Box 310
Shippensburg, PA 17257-0310

*"Speaking to the Purposes of God for this
Generation and for the Generations to Come."*